K. S. (Kaye) Chon
Editor

Tourism in Southeast Asia
A New Direction

Pre-publication
REVIEWS,
COMMENTARIES,
EVALUATIONS . . .

"This book takes a multidisciplinary approach to addressing important tourism planning and development issues faced by Southeast Asian countries. The authors discussed many critical topics tourism planners should consider. The discussions on ecotourism, sustainable development, and environmental impact are particularly timely. The book is a great resource not only for researchers and students in gaining an understanding of this important developing region, but also for Southeast Asian governmental agencies when delineating tourism development directions and strategies. This book is a welcome addition to the limited literature on Southeast Asian tourism."

Cathy H. C. Hsu, PhD
Associate Professor,
Department of Hotel,
Restaurant, Institution
Management and Dietetics,
Kansas State University

The Haworth Hospitality Press®
An Imprint of The Haworth Press, Inc.

Tourism in Southeast Asia
A New Direction

Tourism in Southeast Asia
A New Direction

K. S. (Kaye) Chon
Editor

The Haworth Hospitality Press®
An Imprint of The Haworth Press, Inc.
New York • London • Oxford

Published by

The Haworth Hospitality Press®, an imprint of The Haworth Press, Inc., 10 Alice Street, Binghamton, NY 13904-1580

Cover design by Monica L. Seifert.

Library of Congress Cataloging-in-Publication Data

Tourism in Southeast Asia : a new direction / K. S. (Kaye) Chon, editor.
    p.   cm.
    Includes bibliographical references and index.
    ISBN 0-7890-0732-0 (alk. paper)—ISBN 0-7890-1122-0 (pbk)
    1. Tourism—Asia, Southeastern. I. Chon, K. S. (Kaye)

G155.A743 T683 2000
338.4'791590454—dc21   00-022107

CONTENTS

ABOUT THE EDITOR

K. S. Chon, PhD, CHE, is Professor at the Conrad N. Hilton College of Hotel and Restaurant Management at the University of Houston, Texas. He is also the Executive Editor of the *Journal of Hospitality & Tourism Research,* Editor-in-Chief of the *Journal of Travel & Tourism Marketing* (Haworth), and Editor-in-Chief of the *Asia Pacific Journal of Tourism Research.* In addition, he serves on the editorial review board for numerous scholarly journals in hospitality and tourism, including *Journal of Travel Research, International Journal of Contemporary Hospitality Management, Pacific Tourism Review, Tourism Recreation Research,* and *Journal of Vacation Marketing.*

In 1996, Dr. Chon launched the first Graduate Education and Graduate Students Research Conference in Hospitality and Tourism at the University of Houston. The conference is now an important annual event for graduate students and faculty members who are pursuing research in the field of hospitality and tourism. A former hotel manager and travel industry consultant, Dr. Chon is the author or co-author of over 200 publications, including three books. In 1993, Dr. Chon received the John Wiley & Sons Award from the International Council on Hotel, Restaurant, and Institutional Education (CHRIE) for his lifetime contribution to research and scholarship in hospitality and tourism.

CONTRIBUTORS

Ross K. Dowling is an associate professor of tourism in the School of Marketing, Tourism, and Leisure at Edith Cowan University, Australia. He is vice chairperson of the Forum Advocating Cultural and Ecotourism in Western Australia and Treasurer of the Ecotourism Association of Australia.

John Edmonds is an executive director/Asia-Pacific region for Interval International Inc., a Miami-based vacation exchange company with some 1,600 affiliated resorts worldwide and an individual membership base approaching 1,000,000.

Jutamas Jantarat is a tourism and marketing lecturer at the Department of Business Administration, Prince of Songkla University, Thailand. Her research interests include tourism planning and development, service marketing, and collaborative ventures.

Terry Lam is a senior lecturer in the Department of Hotel and Tourism Management, The Hong Kong Polytechnic University, Hong Kong. His research interests include tourism marketing, development, and hotel industry strategies.

George Leposky is an editor of *Vacation Industry Review,* a trade journal for the timeshare-resort industry. As an adjunct instructor, he has taught courses in timeshare management in the School of Hospitality Management at Florida International University in Miami, Florida.

Connie Mok is an associate professor in the Conrad N. Hilton College of Hotel and Restaurant Management, University of Houston. Her research focuses on consumer behavior in the tourism and hospitality industry.

Alan Nankervis is a senior lecturer in the School of Management, Curtin Business School, Curtin University of Technology, Perth, Western Australia.

Taksina Nimmonratana is an associate professor in tourism at the Faculty of Humanities, Chiang Mai University, Chiang Mai 52000,

Thailand. She received her PhD in tourism from the University of Strathclyde, Glasgow, Scotland.

Bruce R. Prideaux is a lecturer in tourism and transport in the Department of Hospitality, Tourism, and Property Management at The University of Queensland. He is currently completing his PhD on the subject of the causes of development of coastal resorts.

Amrik Singh is an instructor in the Department of Parks, Recreation, and Tourism, University of Utah. He received his master's degree in Hotel Administration from the University of Nevada, Las Vegas.

Dallen J. Timothy is an assistant professor in the School of Human Movement, Sport, and Leisure Studies at Bowling Green State University, Ohio. His research interests include the politics of tourism, international boundaries and tourism, tourism in rural and peripheral regions, tourism planning in developing countries, and heritage tourism.

Lesley Williams is a senior lecturer in marketing at Lincoln University, New Zealand, where she is currently completing a PhD on the impact of culture on marketing. Her other research interests include marketing and management in Southeast Asia, and the influence of culture on international buyer-seller cognition and communication.

Stephen F. Witt is a professor of tourism forecasting at the School of Management Studies for the Service Sector, University of Surrey, United Kingdom. His research focuses on forecasting in tourism and related industries.

Poh Poh Wong is an associate professor in the Department of Geography, National University of Singapore. His publications are mainly in geomorphology, coasts, tourism, and coastal management. He is a member of the International Geographical Union Commission on Coastal Systems.

Preface

Over the last decade, tourist arrivals and receipts in the Asia-Pacific region rose at a rate faster than most parts of the world, almost twice the rates of industrialized countries. Every projection indicates this trend will continue for the next decade and beyond. This book focuses on tourism in Southeast Asia and Indochina, a region that has experienced a remarkable growth in international tourism in recent years. Although the stage of tourism growth and development "life cycle" varies greatly from one country to another, all countries in Southeast Asia and Indochina are facing similar challenges: fostering financially and environmentally sustainable tourism is a common concern. The ten chapters in this book are intended to shed some light on a "new direction" for tourism development, marketing, and management in Southeast Asia and Indochina.

In Chapter 1, Dowling provides a systematic examination of ecotourism efforts in Southeast Asia in general and Thailand in particular. He argues that ecotourism development in Southeast Asia should not be pursued as the panacea for the economic woes of the region but as a tool for fostering the sustainable advancement of local communities. He suggests that ecotourism should be promoted in a manner commensurable with sound environmental practice, cultural preservation, and economic well-being. Relatedly, Edmonds and Leposky in Chapter 3 propose a conceptual framework for the integration of ecotourism and sustainable tourism development and then apply their framework in a case study of tourism development in Sarawak, Malaysia. Last, in Chapter 7, Wong reports on a study on coastal tourism in Southeast Asia with a focus on the environmental preservation perspective. Sustainable tourism development requires a close monitoring of the potential social and cultural impact of tourism. In Chapter 5 (a study of tourism's impacts on the local community in Chiang Mai, Thailand), Taksina

Nimmonratana reports a study in which local residents' perceived impacts of tourism are systematically monitored and analyzed. The author makes some important tourism policy recommendations based on her study.

Timothy, in Chapter 2, examines the issue of cross-border tourism planning and development on an international level in the context of the Association of Southeast Asian Nations (ASEAN). He argues that intergovernmental and regional cooperation need to be promoted in order to facilitate cross-border tourism among Southeast Asian countries. In a related topic (Chapter 6), Prideaux and Witt examine the possible impacts of the recent economic crisis in Southeast Asia on the future development of tourism flows from Australia, a significant market for Southeast Asia's tourism industry. In Chapter 9, Singh sheds some light on the newly emerging segment of the tourism industry in Southeast Asia—the cruise line industry. Singh points out that the viability and future success of the cruise industry will largely depend on the cooperative endeavors of the public and private sectors in each country.

Mok and Lam (Chapter 10) provide insight into Vietnam's tourism industry based on their analysis of the country's tourism potentials and limitations. The authors further provide recommendations for future tourism development and marketing in Vietnam. Jantarat and Williams (Chapter 8) discuss the critical preconditions necessary for the successful coordination of tourism marketing initiatives. Specifically they focus on the critical role of the convener in establishing, legitimizing, and guiding a collaborative tourism activity. Through a case study of the "Amazing Thailand" campaign initiated by the Tourism Authority of Thailand for 1998 and 1999, the authors provide insight into how a campaign convener champions the proposed initiative and persuades stakeholders to participate in a tourism marketing initiative.

I wish to thank the authors who have contributed their important research papers to this volume. Finally, I would like to acknowledge and thank my research assistant, Holly Im, for her editorial contribution, which made the manuscript publishable.

K. S. (Kaye) Chon
University of Houston

Chapter 1

Ecotourism in Southeast Asia: A Golden Opportunity for Local Communities

Ross K. Dowling

INTRODUCTION

Tourism is often promoted as the world's fastest growing industry, and ecotourism is said to be its fastest growing component (*The Economist*, 1998). The tourism potential of natural areas is vast. Reflecting the explosive growth in global ecotourism, a large number of ecotourism organizations and centers have been established (Dowling, 1997a).

Organizations include The Ecotourism Society (TES), a surrogate global ecotourism association based in the United States of America, and the Ecotourism Association of Australia (EAA). Centers include the Institute of Eco-Tourism, Srinakharinwirot University, Bangkok, Thailand; the World Travel and Tourism Research Centre (WRTTRC) in Oxford, England; the International Centre for Ecotourism Research (ICER), Gold Coast, Australia; and the Centre for Ecotourism at the University of Pretoria, South Africa. Tourism, and in particular ecotourism, is growing rapidly in Indonesia, Malaysia, and Thailand. Now many other Southeast Asian nations such as Brunei, Cambodia, Myanmar, and Vietnam are poised to benefit from the emerging popularity of ecotourism.

The author wishes to thank Sarah McNee, Research Assistant, Edith Cowan University, for her contribution to the background research for this chapter.

Ecotourism has been defined as tourism and recreation that is both nature based and sustainable (Lindberg and McKercher, 1997). It is a subset of natural area tourism and may combine elements of both nature-based tourism and adventure travel. However, it is also characterized by a number of other features—notably its educative element and conservation-supporting practice. Five key principles are fundamental to ecotourism: ecotourism is nature based, ecologically sustainable, environmentally educative, locally beneficial, and generates tourist satisfaction (Dowling, 1997b). The first three characteristics are considered essential for a product to be considered "ecotourism" while the last two characteristics are viewed as desirable for all forms of tourism.

Ecotourism has the potential to be a major market segment to be targeted for the expansion and promotion of nature-based tourism resources within the countries of Southeast Asia. It has come to signify an attractive investment proposition, especially in countries at a growing stage of development. Within developing countries it is estimated to earn US$12 billion from an overall US$55 billion in tourism earnings (Davison, 1995). Therefore, ecotourism can provide the economic basis for the conservation and protection of natural areas. Moreover, since many of the natural attractions are located away from urban areas, the potential for regional revitalization exists (Khalifah and Tahir, 1997).

An indication of the commitment to ecologically sustainable tourism within the region is shown by the fact that over 500 Southeast Asian companies exhibited at the eighteenth annual Association of Southeast Asian Nations' (ASEAN) forum on tourism, held on the Philippine Island of Cebu in January 1998. At the conference the three ASEAN travel associations, the Tourism Association, the Federation of Travel Associations, and the Hotel and Restaurant Association, met to discuss plans to improve the quality and sustainability of tourism within the region.

In addition, some Southeast Asian countries are to be commended for the legislation introduced to ensure the protection of the environment. Organizations such as the Pacific Asia Travel Association (PATA) were among the first to develop an environmental ethic (Jansen-Verbeke and Go, 1995). The principles of sustainable tourism are to a large extent expressed in PATA's charter and include strategies for tourism development that benefit both the host country and population. Thus ecotourism is based on the premise espoused by PATA that environmentally responsible policies fully respect the natural and cultural identity of tourism resources.

However, the development of ecotourism has not occurred without difficulties. Frequent problems associated with the advancement of ecotourism within these countries include the lack of infrastructure development, the need for and adequacy of personnel training, the implementation of plans, and political instability.

This chapter now addresses the impacts of ecotourism operations within selected ASEAN countries, focusing on Thailand, and poses the question, Is Southeast Asian ecotourism environmentally appropriate?

ECOTOURISM IN SOUTHEAST ASIA

Issues of ecotourism development in a range of ASEAN countries including Indonesia, Malaysia, Brunei, and Vietnam will be illustrated through a series of selected vignettes in the following sections.

Indonesia

Tourism is of great importance to the Indonesian economy and has been accorded progressively higher priority in the Repelites or five-year plans (Wall, 1997). It is postulated that Indonesia brought ecoawareness to the Southeast Asian region with the 1991 PATA conference, Enrich the Environment, hosted in Bali. Traditionally, tourism within Indonesia has been highly concentrated, focusing on Bali and Jakarta (Gunawan, 1997). Now the country is promoting ecotourism as a major income earner with the government's current policy being to expand tourism from the nation's traditional, developed sites into remote and sometimes sensitive areas. For example, Komodo National Park in eastern Indonesia, the nation's oldest park and home of the world's largest monitor lizard, the Komodo dragon, is keenly seeking tourists. The island is becoming increasingly popular as an ecotourism destination, and the number of visitors has risen from around 3,400 per year in the late 1970s to over 12,000 per year in the early 1990s (Campbell, 1994).

Unfortunately, there is a tendency for investors to capitalize on the ecotourism market regardless of whether or not it is being practiced responsibly. This is illustrated by comparisons of tourism developments in Kuta Bali and Kuta Lombok. Both islands foster ecotourism but have not found an adequate balance among the elements of environmental, economic, and social sustainability.

Wall's (1996) summation of ecotourism development in the two destinations presents an interesting contrast. He concludes that tourism development has taken place rapidly but haphazardly in Kuta Bali in the absence of firm planning guidelines. As a result, the environment appears to be suffering many adverse consequences. In contrast, the more detailed planning in Kuta Lombok has encouraged greater environmental protection. However, he warns that providing an adequate water supply will be challenging in the relatively remote and dry area if substantial development occurs along the southern coast of the island.

Thus Indonesia is facing increased demand for ecotourism and appears to be keen to meet this demand, whatever the cost.

Malaysia

Another country that is progressively marketing ecotourism is Malaysia. As hosts of the XVI Commonwealth Games in 1998, Malaysia launched a year-long global tourism promotion aimed at raising awareness of the country's new sport and leisure facilities. However, most of its attractions are nature based and ecotourism is being heavily promoted.

Malaysia's tropical rainforests are among the oldest and most diverse ecosystems in the world (Khalifah and Tahir, 1997). Current tourist visitation and consequent adverse environmental and social impacts are not a problem, but this situation will have to be monitored, especially with the government's aspiration that by the year 2000 there should be one tourist per head of population.

The Seventh Malaysian Plan is designed to boost the country's tourism industry by popularizing the country's considerable natural attractions (Sadi and Bartels, 1997). The plan promotes ecotourism and is particularly targeted for intensive development. Eligible projects include the construction of new accommodation and recreational facilities. This strategy focuses on eight tourist destinations, most of which are in natural areas. They include Langkawi, Penang, Pangkor, Taman Negara, Malacca, Sarawak, Sabah, and Mount Kinabalu. The plan emphasizes capitalizing on existing attractions and promoting the surrounding tropical hinterlands. For example, in Batang Ai, Sarawak, the development of ecotourism has created employment opportunities for the local villagers and has helped to reduce the hunting pressure on exotic wildlife.

Tourism Malaysia is heavily promoting Sarawak and Sabah as nature and adventure tourism destinations. Recent research at Bako National Park, an established ecotourism destination in Sarawak, clearly identifies some of the negative and positive impacts of ecotourism (Chin, Moore, and Dowling, forthcoming). A survey of 210 visitors indicates that the more common adverse environmental impacts observed include litter, erosion, and damage to vegetation. Specific issues are litter along the beach, soil erosion and vegetation damage along walking trails, the provocation of wildlife, and a lack of enforcement of park regulations.

Most visitors strongly support the following management strategies: educating visitors more about conservation; providing additional directional signs and maps; limiting the overall number of visitors; limiting areas of forest use; and limiting the number of people in a group. Activities participated in by most respondents include photography, hiking, sightseeing, and observation of wildlife.

This study indicates that adverse ecotourism impacts are apparent at Bako National Park, and visitors generally notice their occurrence. The study has important implications not only for Bako's park managers, but also for managers of other national parks in Sarawak because it represents one of the first efforts to address conservation management based on the outcomes of nature tourism.

Robert Basiuk, the managing director of the Kuching-based Borneo Adventure, feels that ecotour operators should focus on providing good guides (Lee, 1996). He suggests that there is a need to raise the minimum standard to ensure that such tours are operated in a manner commensurate with the principles of ecotourism. He suggests that the protection of the natural environment is important if products are to be promoted for the long term. A similar view is shared by David Gill from the National Park and Wildlife Office of Miri's Forest Department. He believes that Sarawak should make it the highest priority to conserve what it has, in particular the rainforest, which is its greatest asset.

Sabah is also being promoted as an ecotourism destination with the recent completion of a number of new accommodation facilities (McNeil, 1997). For example, last year Shangri-La opened a second five-star hotel in Sabah, located on the edge of the rainforest, a forty-minute drive from the capital, Kota Kinabalu. The 330-room hotel has an 18-hole golf course and its own 64-hectare wildlife reserve. Sabah's inbound operation also offers soft adventure activities such as natural history tours, including trips to the Sandakan orangutan sanctuary in the northeast region of the island.

However, despite the growth of ecotourism in Malaysia, concerns for its future have been voiced by Geoffrey Davison, a conservationist with the World Wide Fund for Nature, Malaysia (Lee, 1996). He states that Malaysia has about twenty ecotourism sites, all of which are so overused that new sites will have to be developed; otherwise, ecotourism will become unsustainable. He describes the attention given to ecotourism as slight and patchy and suggests that only a few operators have a credible ecotourism record. Operators have been slow to develop new ecotourism products mainly due to economic constraints and lack of expertise. In addition, profit margins derived from ecotours in the country are slim. To minimize costs some operators have not invested in the research and development of new products.

Brunei

Tourism in Brunei is still in its infancy and it has not yet reached the level of development found in Sarawak and Sabah. However, ecotourism offers the country the promise of sustainable tourism development through its relatively low-impact use of natural resources.

Brunei's newly established tourism unit is currently positioning the country as the gateway to Borneo as a whole because it is considered too small to sell itself as a holiday destination in its own right (McNeil, 1997). Brunei is beginning to work with its neighboring states of Sabah and Sarawak to jointly promote Borneo, and Brunei is the only destination on the island with direct flights from Europe.

The case for fostering ecotourism development in Brunei is suggested as being "particularly attractive and compelling" (Tan, 1995, p. 143). He states that it fits in well with the national policy of keeping the country's land covered by about 80 percent forest. These forests are gazetted for conservation purposes but have much potential for ecotourism, which could also generate economic benefits for the indigenous people. These benefits include establishing markets for their jungle produce and handicrafts and providing services as transport operators, porters, and guides.

In Brunei the development of ecotourism has been spearheaded by the forestry department and various blocks have been converted for recreation. The Batu Apoi Forest Reserve has been converted into a national park. A number of fifty-meter high observation towers have been built, which are linked by some of the longest aerial walkways in the world. In Brunei Bay and in the Belait District additional walkways have been built over mangrove swamps. Observation platforms have been erected in Batang Duri and the S. Liang Arboretum Forest Reserve, and wooden chalets have been built at the beach park in Pantai Sri Kenangan, Tutong (Tan, 1995).

The parks are small and are unable to provide a wide range of ecotourism activities, thus supporting the argument for the establishment of large integrated nature reserves with multifaceted facilities for visitors (Tan, 1995). However, it must be noted that to replace forest production by nature-based ecotourism will not necessarily guarantee sustainability of the natural, cultural, and economic environments.

Vietnam

The Socialist Republic of Vietnam has significant potential for tourism development and it is rich in natural and cultural tourism assets. Its new economic policy of "doi moi" or "openness" is facilitating considerable tourism development, and it was anticipated that the country would attract about 1.5 million international visitors by the year 2000 (Jansen-Verbeke and Go, 1995).

In 1991 a tourism development master plan for Vietnam was published by the World Tourism Organisation (WTO) in collaboration with a United Nations Development Plan. The government has recognized the importance of the development of tourism by making it a priority industry for national development (Cooper, 1997). This has involved preparing a new master plan focusing on infrastructure requirements, education, and the marketing of tourism.

Vietnam has certain advantages as an international tourism destination through its central geographical location in Southeast Asia and its ability to cater to tourists all year round. One of the new tourism concepts proposed is "Vietnam by Train." This will disperse tourism over many regions of the country with minimal environmental impact and low infrastructure costs (Jansen-Verbeke and Go, 1995). A proposal for the future is to build rail links with China and Cambodia.

Tourism development is being concentrated in and around four main economic zones (*Travel and Tourism Intelligence,* 1997). Northern Vietnam is to be developed as the staging area for excursions to Ha Long Bay, with its famous scenery, beaches, and ocean for cruising. The southern part of the central zone has greater potential for ecotourism. There is an abundance of natural resources favoring coastal resort development and consequent nature-based activities in the terrestrial (mountain climbing and rafting) and marine (boating and recreational fishing) environments.

The preservation of the environment is identified as a key issue for this area. For example, there is a need to prevent forest destruction, the pollution of the Perfume River (which flows through Hue) and the Han River (which flows through Danang), and in general the pollution of water, air, and the coastline. Southern Vietnam will particularly foster ecotourism based on the central node of Ho Chi Minh City.

It appears that the Vietnamese government is committed to developing tourism along sustainable guidelines. However, the achievement of this development will be difficult in light of the urgent need for Vietnam to earn foreign exchange and because of its limited resources and knowledge. The issue of sustainability therefore hinges on the political will of the government and the ability of the tourism sector to learn from other countries in the region, which have developed sustainable types of tourism.

Thailand

Thailand is promoting itself as an international destination and the gateway to other Indochinese countries, such as neighboring Vietnam, Myanmar, Cambodia, Malaysia, and Singapore (McNeil, 1997). The government launched the highly successful "Amazing Thailand" campaign in 1998 and 1999. As part of the promotion, cultural performances were held across the country during 1998 and 1999.

Today Thailand is at the forefront of ecotourism development within the Southeast Asian region with the release of its national ecotourism strategy (TAT, 1995). Further enunciation of Thailand's interest is demonstrated by the holding of a large number of eco-tourism conferences within the past three years. These include two international ecotourism conferences hosted by The Institute of Eco-Tourism, Srinakharinwirot University, Bangkok held in February 1995 (Dowling, 1996) and July 1996 (Dowling and Weiler, 1997) and the New Zealand-Thailand Ecotourism Forum held in Bangkok in July 1997.

As part of the "ecopush," the Tourism Authority of Thailand (TAT) is assisting in the design of new hotels to minimize environmental impact. Other measures already undertaken include electrifying Bangkok's "tuk-tuks" (motorcycle taxis) and installing water purification plants to clear Pattaya's beaches.

The push for ecotourism development in Thailand now has the country being marketed as three distinct destination regions—mountains in the north, culture in the center, and beaches in the south (Smith, 1996). Ecotourism issues in each of the three zones are presented next, followed by a specific focus on Phuket.

Northern Thailand

Lisu Lodge in northern Thailand is approximately a one-hour drive from Chiang Mai. It has been upheld as an exemplar in ecotourism building design, environmental interpretation, and community involvement (Muqbil, 1994). Established by John Davies, the lodge plays a central role in the creation of low-density, high-quality ecotours with minimal environmental impact. It promotes exotic experiences for ecotourists while providing the Lisu hill-tribe people with an economic alternative to farming as well as renewed interest and pride in their culture.

Park entrance fees have the potential to contribute directly to management expenses but are currently channeled into the Thai government's general revenues. Doi Inthanon, a national park, world renowned for its "birding" or "du nok," now has a two-tiered fee system, in which foreigners pay a higher amount (US$1.00 compared to $0.20 per person approximately). Recent research in the park indicates that 80 percent of tourists state they are willing to pay more for conservation (http://www.spectrav.com/ecotour thai.html).

Birding is a popular form of ecotourism, but it has the potential to cause adverse environmental impacts. The possibility of the harassment of wildlife is a negative outcome of ecotourism development. For example, some birders attract birds by whistling or playing a tape recorded song, which brings them out into the open to confront the "intruder." However, when used too often, this strategy may cause birds undue stress. Other environmental issues include trampling, litter, and air pollution. Attempts are being made to mitigate these, for example, through the construction of a boardwalk around the summit of Doi Inthanon and through increased tourist awareness of litter and pollution.

One of the key elements of ecotourism is that it should be locally beneficial. Within Doi Inthanon are 600 villages, and the residents earn their living by growing rice and cash crops and through collecting plants and fuelwood for personal use or sale. If hill tribes can benefit economically from ecotourism, they may support habitat protection initiatives and depend less on unsustainable uses of park resources. However, according to Jean Michaud of Montreal University, after a village has been overexposed the tour guides move into newer, more "authentic" territories (Gill and Satyanarayan, 1995). In a similar vein it has been suggested that ecotourism may exacerbate social and cultural impacts by intensifying the degree of contact between hosts and tourists.

Central Thailand

Today 13 percent of the land base of Thailand is environmentally protected. However, efficient management of the protected areas is constrained by low budgets. Attempts to increase the flow of funds have included the construction of resorts within natural areas. This has not always been successful, as demonstrated by occurrences at Khao Yai National Park. In the late 1980s TAT constructed a resort and golf course inside the park. The finding of dead deer that had eaten golf balls, and incidents of elephants killed by falling off steep cliffs after new roads in the park obstructed their normal feeding routes, finally led to the closing down of these projects (Gill and Satyanarayan, 1995).

One of the benefits of ecotourism is that it acts as a model for tourism through the promotion of sustainable development principles, especially in the area of the "greening" of tourism. The Thai Hotel Association is urging its members to "turn green" (Smith, 1996). It has conducted a seminar series on the economic benefits of being "environmentally friendly" and it has implemented a "Green Leaf" program. The Electricity Generating Authority of Thailand has offered interest-free financing to reequip buildings with energy saving equipment. The Tourism Authority of Thailand also helps in the design of new hotels to minimize adverse environmental impacts.

The Marriott Royal Garden Riverside Bangkok and the Royal Garden Resort Hua Hin are exemplars of green practices. The former has an ecocode of ethics and, in addition, fosters environmentally friendly practices outside the immediate hotel environment. Its "Preserve the Kingdom" environmental awareness campaign raises public awareness of some of Thailand's endangered species (http://www.asiatour.com/x-homes/thailand/x-royalgar/royalriv/ecotour.htm).

Southern Thailand

Another model in the field of ecotourism in Thailand is Sea-Canoe International. It is the only internationally acclaimed ecodevelopment laboratory applying innovative economic and management principles to conservation-based, locally owned, rural development (http://www.seacanoe.com). SeaCanoe International began operating canoe expeditions in Phuket after years of operating open sea expeditions on the Pacific Ocean's coastlines. It has a strong environmental protection policy and the company "talks environmentalism to three publics—customers, staff, and the host community" (Gray, 1992, p. 107). The company attributes its success to its commitment to the environment and its requirement of maintaining low tourist volumes. Another key element is SeaCanoe's desire to creatively seek out ecotourism experiences and hence business opportunities.

Siam Safari's Eco-Nature Tours was the first specialist ecotour company to be formed in Phuket. It was founded by Lerd Sun Khomkrit in 1989 and it organizes one- to four-day safaris in southern Thailand. The one-day Phuket Island Eco-Nature Safari by four-wheel drive Land Rover takes visitors off the beaten track, giving four to six people at a time a variety of insights into traditional rural life on the island. The two-day Tropical Rainforest Explorer tour encompasses Khao Sok National Park, 150 kilometers northeast of Phuket on the mainland. The trek in the rainforest with knowledgeable guides offers an opportunity to observe an environment with some of the greatest diversity of life forms on the planet.

In 1996 TAT invested a large sum of money toward developing facilities at Khao Sok National Park. Despite the interest in Khao Sok National Park by the TAT, concerns have been voiced over the lack of apparent control or involvement from the National Parks Division and conservation groups. There are few plans for initiating scientific research or environmental or conservation programs in the park. To date there has been very little research carried out on the flora and fauna of Khao Sok, similarly in other protected areas in Thailand (Dowling and Hardman, 1996). However, if we do not know and understand the resource, we cannot hope to manage it effectively. In addition, if the intricacies and fragile life systems of the park are not understood by scientists, then it stands to reason that the ecotourist will not either.

To overcome this it has been suggested that ecotourism provides a ready-made vehicle for the Royal Forest Department's National Parks Division and the TAT to work together to protect the environment, increase the scientific knowledge of the area, and work with the local community (Hardman, 1997).

Phuket

The tourist destination of Phuket is a microcosm of the issues affecting tourism and the environment in Thailand. Phuket has a history of a litany of tourism-induced environmental problems but also includes some sound examples of tourism-environment symbiosis. For example, in 1992 the Laguna Beach Resort located in Phuket was awarded the International Hotel Association's Environmental Award due to its transformation of a polluted tin mine into an ecosystem of indigenous vegetation that utilizes recycled water, organic waste, and treated sewage (Ayala, 1995).

The International Hotel and Resorts Association 1996 Green Hotelier of the year was awarded to Peter McAlpine, then manager at the Phuket Yacht Club Hotel and Beach Resort. McAlpine's efforts reached beyond the walls of the resort to the wider area of Phuket, a once-pristine island threatened by overdevelopment, mismanagement, and a rapid increase in tourism. His first step was to raise the environmental awareness of the Phuket Yacht Club's 245 employees, organizing staff beach cleanups and tree plantings. Gradually, energy and waste reduction programs were imple-mented. He organized environmental workshops at the hotel and in surrounding villages. With the help of two other hoteliers, he held a bike-a-thon, a cycling fund-raiser.

Hotels in Phuket now have agreed to accept a set of minimum standards for environmental protection. To embrace the flow of ideas, McAlpine hopes to implement a formal structure for ecotourism in Thailand through a system of regional councils. A further initiative is to educate primary schoolteachers in Phuket on enviro-nmentally friendly practices through workshops with follow-up seminars (Shundich, 1997). Largely due to McAlpine's efforts, Phuket has agreed to accept a set of minimum standards for environmental protection, and a resource management act to protect new environmental initiatives is on the government's agenda.

A major survey of the tourism-environment relationship in Phuket has been undertaken in the western bays (Wong, 1995). This study indicates that increased tourism development causes adverse environmental impacts often leading to a complete alteration of the natural environment. However, the increase in tourism pressure continues. For example, United Kingdom long-haul specialist Silk Cut Travel has expanded its program to the Far East with the launch of its 1998 "Hotels of Character" (McNeil, 1997). Over the past two years client feedback has confirmed that the real appeal of the program is the character of the featured hotels combined with locational individuality, management, and atmosphere. In Thailand the operator has reintroduced its resort of Krabi, which it dropped two years ago, and has added hotels in the resorts of Phuket and Ko Samui. Phi Phi Island and northern Thailand itineraries featuring Chiang Mai, Chiang Rai, and the Golden Triangle remain in the program.

An important feature of the tourism industry in Thailand is its close association with ecosystems that have proven to be of only marginal value for other forms of economic activity (Parnwell, 1993). These include the mountain regions of the north as well as the coastal areas of the south. Parnwell's 1993 study of Ko Samui provides an illustration of some of the environmental pressures that have been associated with the relatively unplanned and uncontrolled growth of tourism. Although very small in size, the island is estimated to host a projected 1.1 million visitors annually within two years.

Ko Samui has been vigorously promoted as a major tourism destination by both private sector firms and the Tourism Authority of Thailand. As a consequence, the environment is under increasing pressure from the tourism boom, and the coastline has been changed dramatically. The coral reefs and their associated marine life have come under considerable pressure from scuba diving and souvenir hunting (Parnwell, 1993). This has caused widespread damage to the reefs. So has the large volume of untreated effluent that is discharged into the sea from the island. It is not tourism in itself that is destructive, but rather it is a consequence of the lack of tourism planning and management.

DISCUSSION

The previous examples indicate that Thailand's record of fostering environmentally sensitive tourism development is increasing. However, in addition to the problems cited earlier, others have been noted by Gill and Satyanarayan (1995). They state that with barely 15 to 20 percent of forest area remaining in Thailand, the increasing demands made by ecotourism are now causing intrusions into the last few patches of "unopened" territory. They conclude that Thailand may be entering dangerous territory as watershed areas become exposed and polluted, natural forests are destroyed, and the remaining biodiversity of the country is lost. For example, on Ko Taen the local community has established a conservation club to "conserve the unity of the people and to control the island's tourism to be real ecotourism" (Leksakundilok and Klinsukont, 1997, p. 149).

The theme of the Seventh PATA Adventure Travel and Ecotourism Conference and Mart, held in Balikpapan, East Kalimantan, Indonesia from January 15-18, 1995 was "Nature and Adventure Tourism: Megatrend or Niche." A key outcome was that in order for ecotourism to remain environmentally and socially responsible in the future, it will be necessary to limit tour group size and frequency. Therefore, ecotourism will always remain a "niche" market. Another major issue is the problem of "ecopirates," that is, companies that copy existing responsible tourism products, but operate in a nonresponsible manner (Lew, 1996). Such copies typically offer lower prices, inferior experiences, and detrimental environmental and social impacts.

The advancement of ecotourism in Southeast Asia has obviously had positive and negative impacts on the natural and cultural environments. From a positive perspective, ecotourism fosters a better appreciation of natural environments and their intrinsic and economic worth for protection and conservation. It also provides greater exposure of both the public and governing institutions to nature and conservation, and it also has the potential to motivate the designation of natural areas for conservation and protection.

On the other hand, pressures originating from ecotourism can and do result in degeneration of the very ecosystems on which they depend. Impacts can be particularly severe when there is visitor intrusion where there had been none previously (Wall, 1997). Another important, and often overlooked, factor is that local communities involved in the industry may not have sufficient knowledge to organize a conservation program involving visitor management techniques. Hence they may prioritize visitor satisfaction over the needs of the natural resource (Long, 1991).

In the case of the Southeast Asian countries, extra pressure will be brought to bear to hasten development in order to build up foreign exchange earnings, particularly in the light of current economic crises. Tourism to these countries has never been cheaper; hence, it is envisaged that there will be a large influx of Australian, American, and European travelers. Demand could well outweigh supply and put unsustainable pressure on the environment.

Fostering cruise ship tourism within the region is viewed as one way of bringing in foreign exchange earnings without the necessity of having infrastructure in place and with minimal environmental impact. The cruise industry in the Asia-Pacific region has grown substantially over the recent years and has gained a significant market share in the world's cruise industry. It is the vision of the Singapore government that it become a cruise hub (*Travel Talk,* 1998). From there can be generated an exciting multidestinational ecotourism development program taking in many of the countries of Southeast Asia. The region has so much to offer naturally, historically, and culturally.

CONCLUSION

Earlier this decade it was clear that tourism in Thailand had developed at the expense of its environment (Chon and Singh, 1994) and the question was asked, Is Thailand's tourism boom environmentally sustainable? (Parnwell, 1993, p. 287). The question has as much validity today and can be widened to include the whole Southeast Asian region. Environmental issues in Thailand are still a pressing concern. Despite important gains such as the 1992 Environmental Act, the incapacity of provincial governmental bodies to enforce legislation against polluters and illegal builders in big resorts such as Phuket Island and Pattaya is still evident (Peleggi, 1996).

The extent of ecotourism impacts depends on their efficient detection and identification (either through baseline monitoring of the natural resource or through indicators) and subsequent management actions. Impact identification requires some form of baseline data or indicators to determine acceptable limits of the impacts and changes to the natural environment. Resolving these impacts requires the formulation of management strategies that are able to maintain them at a level that is acceptable for both nature conservation and nature-based recreation.

Tourism and the natural environment can form a symbiotic relationship (Dowling, 1997c). This can be achieved by developing purpose-built tourist resort complexes; investment in and careful design of tourism infrastructure; and hardening sites to carry more tourists while conserving the natural environment. Thus there is a strong case for promoting "sustainable" forms of tourism; such "ecotourism" is a way of fostering harmony between people and nature through tourism. Unfortunately, such principles would appear to be at variance with the economic arguments in favor of mass tourism.

Finally, it is suggested that ecotourism development in Southeast Asia should not be pursued as the panacea for the economic woes caused by the "Asian crisis," but rather viewed as a tool for fostering the sustainable advancement of local communities, in a manner which is commensurate with sound environmental practice, cultural preservation, and economic well-being.

In this way the development of ecotourism in Southeast Asia will advance tourism that is appropriate for the region when based on the principles of community participation and environmental sustainability, a philosophy advocated and pursued by the Thailand Environmental Institute (TEI, 1996).

REFERENCES

Ayala, H. (1995). Ecoresort: A "green" master plan for the international resort industry. *Journal of Hospitality Management* 14(3/4): 351-374.

Campbell, D. (1994). Ecotourism booms in Southeast Asia. *The Ecotourism Society Newsletter* 4(4): 1-3.

Chin, C., Moore, S., and Dowling, R.K. (Forthcoming). Identifying the impacts of ecotourism in the tropics: Bako National Park—a case study.

Chon, K.S. and Singh, A. (1994). Environmental challenges and influences on tourism: The case of Thailand's tourism industry. In Cooper, C.P. and Lockwood, A. (Eds.), *Progress in Tourism, Recreation and Hospitality Management* 6 (pp. 81-91). Chichester: John Wiley & Sons.

Cooper, M. (1997). Tourism planning and education in Vietnam. A profile 1995-2010. *Review* 1: 57-63.

Davison, G. (1995). *Ecotourism in Malaysia: The Present and The Future.* Kuching: Sarawak Tourism Board.

Dowling, R.K. (1996). Ecotourism in Thailand. *Annals of Tourism Research* 23(2): 488-490.

Dowling, R.K. (1997a). The implementation of ecotourism in Australia. In Dhamabutra, P., Stithyudhakarn, V., and Hirunburana, S. (Eds.), *Proceedings of the
Second International Conference on The Implementation of Ecotourism,* Bangkok, Thailand, July 18-21, 1996 (pp. 29-50). Bangkok: The Institute of Eco-
Tourism, Srinakharinwirot University.

Dowling, R.K. (1997b). *National Ecotourism Development Planning.* Proceedings of World Ecotour '97, Rio de Janeiro, Brazil, December 15-18, 1997
(pp. 188-199). Rio de Janeiro: BIOSFERA.

Dowling, R.K. (1997c). Plans for the development of regional ecotourism: Theory
and practice. In Hall, C.M., Jenkins, J., and Kearsley, G. (Eds.), *Tourism Planning
and Policy in Australia and New Zealand: Cases, Issues and Practice* (pp.
110-126). Sydney: Irwin Publishers, McGraw-Hill Book Company.

Dowling, R.K. and Hardman, J. (1996). Ecotourism in Asia: The Thailand experi-
ence. In Richins, H., Richardson, J., and Crabtree, A. (Eds.), *Ecotourism and
Nature-Based Tourism: Taking the Next Steps* (pp. 73-83). Proceedings of The
Ecotourism Association of Australia National Conference 1995. Brisbane: The
Ecotourism Association of Australia.

Dowling, R.K. and Weiler, B. (1997). Ecotourism in South East Asia. *Tourism
Management* 18(1): 51-53.

The Economist (1998). Dream factories: A survey of travel and tourism. *The
Economist,* January 10, pp. 13-16.

Gill, T. and Satyanarayan, S. (1995). Critics see downside to Thai-style ecotourism. *The Nation,* February 12, p. 12.

Gray, J. (1992). Earth first can be good business. In Hay, J.E. (Ed.), *Promoting a
Sustainable Experience.* Proceedings of the Ecotourism Conference, held at
the University of Auckland, October 12-14, 1992 (pp. 107-110). Auckland:
Environmental Science, University of Auckland.

Gunawan, M.P. (1997). National planning for Indonesia's tourism. *Pacific Tourism Review* 1: 47-56.

Hall, C.M. (1997). *Tourism in the Pacific Rim: Developments, Impacts and Markets,* Second edition. Melbourne: Longman Australia.

Hardman, J. (1997). Ecotourism in Khao Sok National Park. In Dhamabutra, P.,
Stithyudhakarn, V., and Hirunburana, S. (Eds.), *Proceedings of the Second
International Conference on The Implementation of Ecotourism* (pp. 216-224).
Bangkok: Institute of Eco-Tourism, Srinakharinwirot University.

Jansen-Verbeke, M., and Go, F. (1995). Tourism development in Vietnam. *Tourism Management* 16(4): 315-325.

Khalifah, Z. and Tahir, S. (1997). Malaysia: Tourism in perspective. In Go, F.M.,
and Jenkins, C.L. (Eds.). *Tourism and Economic Development in Asia and
Australasia* (pp. 176-196). London: Cassell.

Lee, M. (1996). A long way to go. *PATA Travel News,* May, p. 12.

Leksakundilok, A. and Klinsukont, C. (1997). The ecotourism establishment in a
small island: Ko Taen. In Dhamabutra, P., Stithyudhakarn, V., and Hirunburana, S. (Eds.), *Proceedings of the Second International Conference on The*

Implementation of Ecotourism (pp. 149-160). Bangkok: Institute of Eco-Tourism, Srinakharinwirot University.

Lew, A. (1996). Adventure travel and ecotourism in Asia. *Annals of Tourism Research* 23(3): 723-724.

Li, L. and Zhang, W. (1997). Thailand: The dynamic growth of Thai tourism. In Go, M.F. and Jenkins, C.L. (Eds.), *Tourism and Economic Development in Asia and Australasia* (pp. 286-303). London: Cassell.

Lindberg, K. and McKercher, B. (1997). Ecotourism: A critical overview. *Pacific Tourism Review* 1: 65-79.

Long, V.H. (1991). Nature tourism: Environmental stress or environmental salvation? In Veal, A.J., Johnson, P., and Cushman, G. (Eds.), *Leisure and Tourism: Social and Environmental Change.* Papers presented from the World Leisure and Recreation Association Congress, Sydney, Australia, July 16-19, 1991 (pp. 615-623). Lindfield: Centre for Leisure and Tourism Studies, University of Sydney.

Marriott Royal Garden Riverside Bangkok, Thailand <http://www.asiatour.com/x-homes/thailand/x-royalgar/royalriv/ecotour.htm>.

McNeil, L. (1997). Sports facilities the main focus as Commonwealth Games draw near. *Travel Weekly,* November 12, pp. 76-86.

Muqbil, I. (1994). Lessons from the Lisu. *PATA Travel News,* March, pp. 12-15.

NZ helps Thai ecotourism efforts in unique forum. Bangkok, Thailand, July 31, 1997 <http://www.tourismthailand.org/news/tat_nztb.htm>.

Parnwell, M.J.G. (1993). Environmental issues and tourism in Thailand. In Hitchcock, M., King, V.T., and Parnwell, M.J.G. (Eds.), *Tourism in Southeast Asia* (pp. 286-302). London: Routledge.

Peleggi, M. (1996). National heritage and global tourism in Thailand. *Annals of Tourism Research* 23(2): 432-448.

Petry, J. (1996, May). Northern exposure. *PATA Travel News,* p. 10.

Royal Garden Resort Hua Hin <http://www.asiatour.com/x-homes/thailand/x-royalgar/royalhua/ecotour.htm>.

Sadi, M.A. and Bartels, F.L. (1997). The rise of Malaysia's tourism industry: Implications for Singapore. *Cornell HRA Quarterly* 38(5): 88-95.

SeaCanoe <http://www.seacanoe.com>.

See-Tho, E.K. (1996). Mother nature earns a buck. *PATA Travel News,* May, pp. 6-9.

Shundich, S. (1997). Champions of green hotel keeping. *Hotels* 31(3): 49-54.

Smith, K. (1996). The three faces of Thailand. *Travel Talk Asia-Pacific,* May 23-June 20, pp. 35-42.

Tan, P.K. (1995). A case for ecotourism development in Brunei Darussalam. *Malaysian Journal of Tropical Geography* 26(2): 143-149.

TAT (1995). *Policies and Guidelines: Development of Ecotourism (1995-1996) of the Tourism Authority of Thailand.* Bangkok: Tourism Authority of Thailand.

TEI (1996). *Towards Environmental Sustainability.* Thailand Environmental Institute, Annual Report. Bangkok: Thailand Environmental Institute.

Travel and Tourism Intelligence (1997). International tourism reports—Vietnam. *Travel and Tourism Intelligence* 2: 79-102.

Travel Talk (1998). Cruise report. *Travel Talk,* December 23-January 28, p. 414.

Wall, G. (1996). One name, two destinations: Planned and unplanned coastal resorts in Indonesia. In Harrison, L., and Husbands, W. (Eds.), *Practicing Responsible Tourism: International Case Studies in Tourism Planning, Policy, and Development* (pp. 41-57). New York: John Wiley & Sons Inc.

Wall, G. (1997). Indonesia: The impact of regionalization. In Go, M.F., and Jenkins, C.L. (Eds.), *Tourism and Economic Development in Asia and Australasia* (pp. 138-149). London: Cassell.

Wong, P.P. (1995). Tourism environment interaction in the western bays of Phuket Island. *Malaysian Journal of Tropical Geography* 26(1): 67-75.

Wong, P.P. (1997). Tourism planning and education in Vietnam. A profile 1995-2010. *Pacific Tourism Review* 1: 57-63.

Chapter 2

Tourism Planning in Southeast Asia: Bringing Down Borders Through Cooperation

Dallen J. Timothy

INTRODUCTION

Political boundaries have traditionally functioned as barriers to human interaction. Government policies and borders, which mark the limits of national sovereignty, have acted to control the flow of goods, people, and services between countries. During the past decade, however, the world has undergone tremendous geopolitical changes, wherein the role of political frontiers has become that of a line of integration rather than simply a barrier to interaction. Liberalization of trade policies, the easing of travel restrictions by many countries, and international cooperation in economic development have been at the forefront of these shifts in political ideologies. These changes have had significant impacts on international tourism, including a widespread decrease in the traditional barrier effects of international boundaries in terms of the flow of people and trade in goods and services. Although the concept of international cooperation in tourism planning is new and not yet widespread, some international destination regions, such as the United States and Canada (Richard, 1993) and Jordan and Israel (Kliot, 1996), are beginning to realize the value of working together to develop and promote common tourism resources.

Many of these political changes have been closely associated with the establishment of strategic alliances and international economic communities, such as the Association of Southeast Asian Nations

(ASEAN), the European Union (EU), and the North American Free Trade Agreement (NAFTA). Although none of these alliances has tourism development as its primary goal, such coalitions do facilitate the regionalization of tourism on an international level and tend to increase tourism's supply and demand bases (Timothy, 1995a, 1995b).

In areas where tourism resources are shared by two or more autonomous political entities, at any level (e.g., national, provincial, county), efficient and integrative planning can be achieved best through cooperative efforts. As with other aspects of tourism, tourism planning and development have been traditionally restricted by political borders in most countries and regions. However, tourism planning on international and cross-border subnational levels has recently been recognized as a means of developing more sustainable forms of tourism that promote principles such as equity, efficiency, ecological integrity, balance, and harmony (Wall, 1993; Bramwell and Lane, 1993; Timothy, 1999). Transboundary cooperation is now also beginning to be viewed as a way of improving mutual economic benefits and political relations between neighbors (Timothy, 1998).

This chapter is concerned with international cooperation in Southeast Asia. The types and levels of cooperation in ASEAN and subregional growth triangles are examined, and obstacles to cooperative planning are considered in each situation.

ASEAN COOPERATION

The formation of ASEAN in 1967 was primarily a response to the threat of communism in Southeast Asia during the 1960s. The organization's member nations at that time—Thailand, Singapore, Malaysia, the Philippines, and Indonesia (Brunei joined the organization after its independence from Britain in 1984)—feared that they might be overrun by communist forces, so they united in an effort to avoid foreign occupation (Hagiwara, 1973; Tasker, Schwarz, and Vatikiotis, 1994).

The primary aims of ASEAN were to ensure peace and stability in the region, to promote and facilitate intraregional economic development, and to encourage social and cultural progress among members (Hussey, 1991, p. 87). Much of the function of the association during its early years was merely symbolic. However, by the middle of the 1970s, after the withdrawal of the United States from Indochina and the establishment of communist governments in the region, members of ASEAN hastened to renew their commitment to the organization (Hussey, 1991; Stockwin, 1975). In 1976 the first ASEAN Summit was held in Bali, Indonesia, where the primary topic of discussion was economics (Broinowski, 1982). At the summit, the Treaty of Amity and Cooperation in Southeast Asia was signed, and the heads of government of all member countries agreed to strengthen economic cooperation and mutual assistance (Castro, 1982). Since that time, most of ASEAN's initiatives have centered on economic cooperation and culture, and less on issues of security.

In recent years, the organization has been under increasing internal and external pressures to widen its role, especially in terms of taking more responsibility for regional security, accepting new members (e.g., Vietnam and Laos), and expediting the growth of business and trade links among members (Tasker, Schwarz, and Vatikiotis, 1994). Pressures from within to implement integration more quickly originate mostly from the private sector. Presently, one of ASEAN's primary goals is to establish the ASEAN Free Trade Area (AFTA), a program that aims to reduce internal tariffs significantly within the next decade.

Intra-ASEAN trade has long been dominated by minerals and fuels (Hussey, 1991). However, recent years have seen the rise of tourism as one economic focus of the association. This is in large part owing to the fact that tourism in the region has grown so rapidly since 1980. Much of this growth can be attributed to increasing personal and national affluence in Southeast Asia and the improved accessibility of ASEAN to the tourist markets in the developed West and Japan (Min, 1980). Significant improvements to the tourism infrastructure and more intensive, worldwide promotional efforts on the part of all member countries except Brunei have also contributed to this growth.

In 1980, 7.03 million foreign tourists arrived in ASEAN countries. Only ten years later, in 1990, that number had nearly tripled to 21.03 million. By 1994, the number of foreign arrival in ASEAN had reached nearly 26 million. Southeast Asia is in fact one of the fastest growing regions for tourism globally, in terms of both intra-ASEAN travel and travel to the region from other parts of the world (Hall, 1994). However, natural disasters, plane crashes, and the current economic crisis in the region contributed to a decrease in international arrivals in 1997 (*Jakarta Post,* 1998). Estimates by the International Air Transport Association (IATA) predict that international air traffic to the ASEAN region will reach 189 million passengers by the year 2000 and will double again in 2010 (*Travel Indonesia,* 1994). Japan is the region's largest external market, followed by Taiwan, Hong Kong, Korea, Europe, and the Americas (Hall, 1994), while the region's largest overall market is itself (*Travel Indonesia,* 1991, 1994).

Although ASEAN is considered by many observers to be the most successful international alliance among developing countries (Imada, Montes, and Naya, 1991), many critics suggest that the organization's achievements in the area of regional economic cooperation, including tourism, have been uneven and weak (Hussey, 1991; Naidu, 1988; Wong, 1989). Few efforts to improve economic cooperation have been successful.

Although members of ASEAN have been involved in relatively few areas of close cooperation and tend to form their own national policies regarding economic development, a few examples exist where cooperation has been achieved in areas related to tourism. For example, when the association began to realize the importance of tourism in Southeast Asia, the Sub-Committee on Tourism (SCOT) was established and charged with arranging cooperation in marketing the region as a single destination. Although SCOT was dissolved in the mid-1990s, it is viewed as an early attempt to initiate cooperative efforts. Related endeavors, such as the recent establishment of ASEAN Tourism Association (ASEANTA), demonstrate a continued interest in the promotional aspects of tourism planning.

Most ASEAN cooperation in tourism has so far been relegated to promotion and marketing. Over ten years ago, Wong (1987) outlined several areas wherein ASEAN member states have cooperated in tourism (see Table 2.1). Although these examples are mostly from the 1980s, little additional cooperation has occurred since then. One exception was the designation of 1992 as Visit ASEAN Year. Following the successful efforts of Thailand to promote Visit

TABLE 2.1. Past ASEAN Cooperative Efforts in Tourism Development

Endeavor	Description
ASEAN Travel Information Centre	Established in Kuala Lumpur as SCOT's permanent secretariat. Its job is to coordinate and manage ASEAN marketing programs and to act as liaison with other international tourism bodies.
ASEAN tourism fora	Since 1981, these have been held every three years as a venue for tourism workshops and markets where ASEAN sellers of tourism meet foreign buyers. Organized and funded by ASEAN NTOs.
ASEAN promotional chapters	Six ASEAN chapters act as SCOT's promotional arms in major tourist markets: Japan, Australia, Hong Kong, UK, and the United States.
Collective representation	ASEAN NTOs periodically attend world travel markets collectively to project a common ASEAN image.
ASEAN travel films and brochure	ASEAN countries have combined resources to produce travel films and brochures.
Research and human resource training	Workshops have been conducted to discuss common tourism terminologies for data collection to facilitate information exchange among ASEAN countries, and to discuss tourism training needs.

Source: Adapted from Wong, 1987.

Thailand Year in 1987, the ASEAN government tourist boards agreed to promote their countries in succession, culminating in a joint venture in 1992 to involve the entire region (Hitchcock, King, and Parnwell, 1993; Walton, 1993). Through SCOT, the ASEAN countries worked together to promote all member countries as one destination, to encourage overseas visitors to remain longer through the promotion of multidestination vacations, and to offer special air travel incentives. Japan, Australia, Germany, and the ASEAN region itself were targeted as the principal markets. The campaign slogan, "ASEAN—the World's Only 6-in-1 Tropical Paradise," was adopted. Given vigorous promotion by government tourist boards, SCOT was expected to bring in a target of 22 million tourists for Visit ASEAN Year. In fact, their efforts were fruitful, but visitor numbers fell short of the goal by nearly 800,000. Lingering effects of the Gulf War no doubt contributed to this shortfall.

Regardless of these initial efforts toward international cooperation in tourism marketing planning, they are still the exception rather than the rule. Relatively few examples of cooperation in tourism planning and development throughout ASEAN exist today in important areas such as human resources, conservation, and infrastructure development (Timothy, 1999). However, recent plans on the part of the Thai government to begin privatizing Thai Airways and Bangkok's international airport will very likely result in more cooperation. Plans to create border-free air space in Southeast Asia, recently proposed laws to initiate a customs-free zone, and a 1997 memorandum of understanding among ASEAN nations for cooperation in services (Panitchapat, 1998) are good examples of recent worthwhile attempts to bring down barriers through cooperation.

CONSTRAINTS ON CROSS-BORDER COOPERATION IN ASEAN

One reason for a general lack of intra-ASEAN cooperation is that the economic structures of individual ASEAN member countries are competitive rather than complementary (Hussey, 1991; Imada, Montes, and Naya, 1991). In terms of tourism specifically, the structure of ASEAN tourism is not conducive to regional cooperation. Tourism in each country is essentially self-contained (Hussey, 1991). Few cross-border ties have existed in the past, and few exist today. In common with other economic sectors, tourism tends to be competitive rather than complementary, as most countries in the region offer similar tourism resources: cultural heritage, sun, and inexpensive shopping. Consequently, member countries are focusing their promotional efforts on the same target markets: residents of Western, industrialized nations.

Several political issues can also be blamed for a lack of regional cooperation in tourism planning. According to Pangestu, Soesastro, and Ahmad (1992), the most significant underlying barrier to the actualization of ASEAN economic cooperation has been a lack of political commitment. Nontariff barriers, such as licensing, prohibitions, and import quotas, are employed by individual countries to protect domestic economies (Hussey, 1991). This obviously restricts the degree to which the economies of member states can be integrated. Individual national governments are reluctant to alter these types of trade policies, and they have consciously avoided participating in any significant way in market-sharing agreements. Political problems also arise from the fact that ASEAN leaders have tended to concern themselves only with broad regional programs, leaving the implementation of regional dec'sions to officials of individual countries (Wong, 1989). Other political problems exist, which place significant barriers in the way of tourism and other forms of economic cooperation. Although they were more significant in the past, arguments between members over fishing rights still occur. Furthermore, several heated disputes over territorial boundaries on land between member states and questions of ownership of the Spratly Islands have not yet been resolved, even though attempts have been made by some member countries to develop tourism on the islands in order to legitimize their territorial claims.

According to some observers, colonialism is another political factor that affects cooperative efforts in the region. McCloud (1995, p. 301) claims that the region's colonial history "further fractured the region while artificially integrating the fractured pieces into the global system." This heritage, together with traditional systems, has led to a system of conflict, rather than one of cooperation (McCloud, 1995).

That the economies of ASEAN states are at different levels of development and therefore are not as compatible as members of the European Union, who are essentially all at high levels of economic development (Alburo, 1990; Hussey, 1991; Wong, 1989), may also be an obstacle to regional cooperation in tourism planning. Most of the less-developed members of ASEAN are more concerned with domestic problems, such as unemployment and poverty, than they are with international issues. As Wong (1989) pointed out, the

less-developed members cannot rely on external economic cooperation programs to deal with their internal economic problems.

Finally, the transportation components of tourism in ASEAN have
been hindered by a lack of coherent regional objectives and by the
fact that national priorities are dominant in each country. Regional
cooperation usually means increased competition for the transport
sector of each state. There does appear to be a lack of commitment
and enthusiasm on the part of ASEAN governments for cooperative
planning in transportation. This reflects national priorities that super-
cede regional considerations (Naidu, 1988), a problem common to
many international communities (e.g., NAFTA).

THE GROWTH TRIANGLE

The concept of a growth triangle originated in, 1989, when Singapore declared its intentions to invite the Indonesian province of
Riau and Malaysia's Johor state to join forces in a sub-ASEAN
economic alliance (see Figure 2.1). In 1990, Indonesia and Malaysia both endorsed the growth triangle concept.

One goal of the triangle was to strengthen economic and social
links between Singapore, Indonesia, and Malaysia, including joint
promotion of the area as an investment site for multinational corpo-
rations. Another goal was to decrease the barrier effects of member
countries' state borders by facilitating greater flows of capital,
goods, and labor across international frontiers (Parsonage, 1992).
Tyler (1992) claimed that the overriding goal of the alliance, however, was to provide mutually beneficial growth between the three
states by taking advantage of regional economic disparities, since
this obviously was more difficult to achieve on an ASEAN-wide
basis.

The Singapore-Johor-Riau Growth Triangle is the first of its kind
and is often cited as a model for other emergent subregional
associations. Several other growth triangles are in the early planning stages in Southeast Asia, including one between North Sumatra (Indonesia), four of Malaysia's northern states, and Thailand's
five southern provinces (Radio Thailand, 1995), as well as East
Malaysia, Sulawesi and Kalimantan in Indonesia, and parts of the
Philippines (Ramos, 1995).

FIGURE 2.1. The Singapore-Johor-Riau Growth Triangle

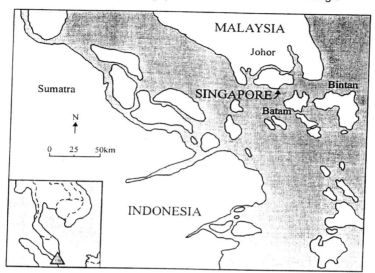

According to Ramos (1995, p. 12), "The growth triangle concept has taken hold because it is a controlled experiment in regional cooperation whose adverse effects, if any, can be limited to the triangle, but whose beneficial results can subsequently be applied to the national economy as a whole."

A shortage of land and a dearth of labor supply drove Singapore to seek some form of economic cooperation with neighboring regions of Malaysia and Indonesia. From Singapore's perspective, the competitive advantages among the three parties are complementary. Singapore has a highly developed infrastructure, an abundance of qualified human resources, and high levels of capital. Johor has land and semiskilled labor. Riau has cheap land and low-cost labor (Kumar and Yuan, 1991).

Prior to the formation of the three-way alliance, the economic relationship between Singapore and Johor state was already well-established. Owing to its proximity to Singapore, Johor was seen in Malaysia as a significant growth center for the entire country. Nearly half of Singapore's trade with Malaysia passed through Johor, and since around 70 percent of Malaysia's tourist arrivals enter the country from Singapore, Johor was seen as a major tourist gateway as well (Parsonage, 1992). Most of Singapore's water is supplied by Johor, and many of the state's industrial developments were financed by Singaporean investors. Furthermore, many Singapore-based industries moved to Johor to take advantage of lower labor and real estate costs compared to those at home.

In 1970, Batam, the first of the Riau islands to be developed, was designated a strategic base for oil and gas, and Indonesia's plan was to build an industrial region that could compete with Singapore (Tyler, 1992). In 1978, duty-free status was extended across the whole island in an attempt to stimulate growth. In addition to oil and gas, other industries, such as warehousing, transshipment, and tourism were targeted (Milne, 1993; Perry, 1991). In 1989, a memorandum of understanding was signed between Singapore and Indonesia to reduce administrative barriers to intraregional investment, which was supposed to foster joint participation in the development of infrastructure and marketing of the region (Perry, 1991). Through this agreement, 100 percent foreign ownership became possible in Batam for five years, after which only 5 percent was to be transferred to Indonesian investors. Until this time, foreign ownership was not permitted. This breakthrough in investment policy prompted the formation of a Singapore-Indonesia joint venture to develop an industrial estate, the Batam Industrial Park, for international investment.

Singapore has played the most significant role in transforming Batam's economy. In 1990 it accounted for nearly 45 percent of the cumulative foreign investments in Batam. Furthermore, the largely Singapore-backed Batam Industrial Development Authority commenced upgrading the island's infrastructure in the early 1990s, including an expansion of airport capacity, a deep-water cargo terminal, and the development of a commercial center (Perry, 1991).

Critics of the growth triangle claim that Singapore is the main beneficiary of this arrangement. However, proponents stress that Malaysia and Indonesia will benefit from increased employment opportunities and foreign exchange, as well as Singapore's capital support, management expertise, and better communications and transportation facilities that offer better access to the world. Some observers suggest that the primary benefits for Johor and Batam from this three-way cooperative effort will be related to tourism. Kamil, Pangestu, and Fredericks (1991), for example, maintained that both regions would enjoy higher levels of spillover from tourists who visit Singapore.

With the apparent success of industrial development on Batam, other islands were selected for additional development. Bintan, just to the east of Batam and ten minutes farther from Singapore by ferry boat, was selected to become the focus of joint Indonesian-Singaporean efforts to develop a major resort complex over the next two decades. With this designation, tourism investments and development efforts in the Riau islands shifted to Bintan.

Most tourism development by Singapore in Johor has been related directly to meeting the needs of Singaporean tourists. Recent efforts in Bintan, however, reflect Singapore's desire to attract not only Singaporean travelers, but also international tourists who visit the island, to its resorts in neighboring Indonesia, in effect expanding its tourism hinterland.

Singapore's involvement in Batam and Bintan was formalized by agreement in, 1990, which opens the way toward increased binational development of tourism (Parsonage, 1992). This arrangement has created a whole new level of cooperation between Singapore and Indonesia. Extensive efforts are currently under way by both governments to promote internationally the concept of urban, historic, consumer-oriented Singapore and its exotic, relaxing, and scenic sidekick, Bintan. Much of the current promotional material is a joint effort and reflects this new approach. For example, the cover of one brochure attempts to seize the attention of potential international travelers: "Experience Singapore and Bintan, 2 Worlds, 45 Minutes Apart." The same brochure claims, "For an experience that combines the best of both worlds, Singapore and Indonesia's Bintan Island is what you've been waiting for" and "Shop to your heart's content in Singapore's sophisticated Orchard Road, then let your heartbeat slow to the rhythm of the waves lapping Bintan's shores" (Singapore Tourist Promotion Board/Bintan Resort Management Ltd., n.d.).

Tremendous efforts are currently under way to develop a 23,000-hectare resort complex on Bintan's north coast, which is expected to be completed in fifteen to twenty years at an estimated cost of $3.5 billion Singapore dollars (Wee, 1996). The Bintan Resorts Company, a joint Singapore-Indonesia venture, recently sold a 450-hectare site to an American developer for the building of a large beach resort. Several resorts are already operational and several more are still in the planning phases. Golf courses have already been built, and proposed future developments include an amusement park, a marina, nature-based tours, and agro-tourism parks where tourists can pick their own fruits and vegetables. Other parts of the resort complex will be divided into ten or twenty small lots of up to twenty hectares each, which will be sold to small investors for developing guest houses or two- and three-star hotels (Wong, 1996).

Promotional efforts for Bintan are geared toward residents of Singapore. Thousands of Singaporeans are eager to discover new weekend destinations, just to get away from the island's crowded conditions. As mentioned above, the resort is also being promoted to international visitors in conjunction with Singapore. The proximity to Singapore's Changi Airport and a mere forty-five-minute ferry ride make Bintan easily accessible to international tourists as well (Wee, 1996).

In 1993, Riau received 931,427 international visitors. Most of these were concentrated in Batam and Bintan—an area that had received only 579,300 tourists in 1990 (Directorate General of Tourism, 1994). The existence of major tourism developments on Batam and Bintan Islands, with frequent ferry connections to Singapore, accounts for this region's high number of international arrivals.

The planned Bintan beach resorts are expected to help Singapore overcome its limitations of land, natural resources, and labor. At the same time, Indonesia will benefit from increased capital flows, large foreign exchange earnings, increased employment, and greater business opportunities (*Business Times,* 1996; Hoong, 1996).

Despite the progress made so far in the triangle, even in terms of tourism, the three governments involved have been reluctant to conclude a formal tripartite agreement that would institutionalize it (Milne, 1993). Thus far, the only formal agreements among triangle members have been between Indonesia and Singapore. Johor appears to have been left in the shadows of the triangle's rapid tourism development efforts. The core of recent tourism cooperation has been between Bintan and Singapore; however, cooperation between Singapore and Johor remains strong, and Johor is still an important destination for Singaporeans.

Although the three countries involved in the growth triangle have met with some degree of successful cooperation, as is evident from the preceding discussion, they do not appear to be functioning together in a tripartite system. Several obstacles exist, which prevent the growth triangle concept from working as it was originally envisioned. This lack of trinational cooperation has led to the Malaysian and Indonesian views that it is actually the Singapore-Riau and Singapore-Johor linkages that exist. The Johor-Riau connection hardly exists at all (Pangestu, 1991; Kamil, Pangestu, and Fredericks, 1991). "To be sure, Johor and Riau are seldom in competition, with the partial exception of electronics. But neither are they complementary. They simply have little to do with each other directly. Even the ferry between Johor and Bintan is routed via Singapore" (Milne, 1993, p. 293). Ooi (1995, p. 344) summarizes the situation as follows: "Certainly the triangular or trilateral agreement appears to have seen more linkage on a bilateral basis, that is, between Johor and Singapore and similarly between Singapore and Riau Islands. There is as yet little evidence of the development of three-way links between the countries involved in the growth triangle."

CONSTRAINTS ON THREE-WAY COOPERATION IN THE GROWTH TRIANGLE

Overall, Indonesia has been a willing partner in the proposed three-way alliance. Malaysia, on the other hand, has demonstrated a less energetic role in the partnership. According to political observers, this is a result of ongoing disagreements between the federal government and the Johor state government (Milne, 1993). Constitutionally, the government of Johor cannot make decisions pertaining to international affairs without federal government approval, except in cases of land, religion, and Malay culture. This has been a major point of contention between the state and federal government in that state's efforts to become a more active member of the growth triangle. The Johor state administration is clearly in favor of the triangle, but it is required to wait for approval and action on the part of the federal government (Kamil, Pangestu, and Fredericks, 1991, p. 63). The federal government is reluctant because the relationships that exist are between regions (e.g., Johor state and Riau province) rather than independent nations. Johor is already one of Malaysia's fastest-growing states, and federal bureaucrats fear that the growth triangle would accentuate this pattern and conflict with national aims to spread economic development to other parts of the country (Perry, 1991). Furthermore, Johor is not a duty-free zone, as are Singapore, Batam, and Bintan, and it is unlikely to become such because of the difficulty of policing the border into the rest of Malaysia (Ooi, 1995; Perry, 1991). These concerns of national-level authorities result in delayed action and frustration on the part of Johor.

The Indonesian government, however, has been much more flexible in its part of the triangular relationship. That country's development goals also include spreading the economic benefits of tourism to the peripheral regions of the country, away from the traditional centers of tourism, such as Java and Bali. Since Riau is on the country's geographic and economic periphery, as opposed to the place of Johor in Malaysia, tourism and other economic activities fit comfortably into national goals for economic development.

Another obstacle is that the complementarity of the three neighbors is limited. This is most obvious in Johor, whose economic aspirations increasingly challenge Singapore (Perry, 1991). Complementarity is most apparent in the Singapore-Riau relationship.

Tensions also exist in Johor in relation to Singapore that limit the two parties' full participation in the triangle. Recent years have brought about a rapid increase in the local cost of living in terms of real estate and goods and services, owing largely to business investments in the state by Singapore-based companies and Singaporean tourists who cross the border to shop.

Congestion at border crossings and stringent immigration procedures also act as major deterrents for tourism between Malaysia and Singapore (Perry, 1991). A second causeway between the two countries is in the works, which will decrease crowded conditions at the border. Although loosening immigration and customs controls between the two countries has been considered, border-crossing formalities are still relatively stringent.

In Batam and Bintan, however, the infrastructure has been developed significantly, so that more tourism connections exist between Singapore and the Riau Islands. New ferry services and better roads have increased accessibility to and within the islands. Furthermore, as mentioned earlier, investment rules and immigration and customs procedures have been eased between Singapore and Indonesia's islands, which allows a greater degree of cooperation between the two regions.

CONCLUSION

This chapter has examined the concept of cross-border cooperation in tourism planning and development in Southeast Asia. Cooperative efforts between countries or provinces can be instrumental in promoting principles of sustainable tourism development, such as efficiency, equity, harmony, and integrative regional tourism planning.

Owing to the region's fragmented political traditions, economic disparities between nations, and each country's unwillingness to decrease barriers to trade and immigration, few cooperative efforts have succeeded in ASEAN so far, and the goal of the Singapore-Johor-Riau Growth Triangle for equal partnership has not yet been realized. Nevertheless, smaller-scale cooperation within the growth triangle has been more successful than efforts among the wide range of diverse countries that make up ASEAN.

In the two cases examined in this paper, the few incidents of cooperation that exist are mostly examples of promotion and marketing. Although these are very important in regional planning, other areas of concern also need to be addressed: cooperation in human resource management, nature and heritage conservation, and infrastructure development. The development of multination travel packages and true borderless regional promotion would at least begin to alleviate some of the economic disparities between neighboring countries. Standardizing tourism services and undertaking joint training programs and exchange arrangements would also encourage greater levels of cooperation.

Perhaps the most important issue that needs to be addressed, however, is political will and the opening up of political boundaries to allow a freer cross-border movement of goods, services, and people in Southeast Asia. The traditional nature of political boundaries as barriers to interaction must be replaced, at least in part, by a new perspective that views borders as lines of integration. Although this is easier said than done, it is important if regional goals for cooperation in tourism are to be met, as they have been in other international economic alliances throughout the world. In this way, complementarity between adjacent regions can be created.

Although this chapter has focused on the traditional difficulties of regional cooperation in Southeast Asia, conditions are changing, and there appears to be a growing desire among ASEAN leaders to promote regional economic cooperation. This is clear from recent movements to create the ASEAN Free Trade Area and to promote cooperation in services. As Thai member of parliament Tawat Wichaidit declared in his 1998 keynote address at a recent conference, "There is no longer one country that can survive tourism development alone in this region."

REFERENCES

Alburo, F.A. (1990). The ASEAN Summit and ASEAN economic cooperation. In S. Naya and A. Takayama (Eds.), *Economic Development in East and Southeast Asia: Essays in Honor of Professor Shinichi Ichimural* (pp. 300-305). Singapore: Institute of Southeast Asian Studies.

Bramwell, B. and Lane, B. (1993). Sustainable tourism: An evolving global approach. *Journal of Sustainable Tourism* 1(1): 1-5.

Broinowski, A. (Ed.) (1982). *Understanding ASEAN*. New York: St. Martin's Press.

Business Times (1996). S'pore, Indonesia launches tropical island resort. *Business Times,* June 3.

Castro, A. (1982). ASEAN Economic Co-operation. In A. Broinowski (Ed.), *Understanding ASEAN* (pp. 70-91). New York: St. Martin's Press.

Directorate General of Tourism (1994). Unpublished seminar notes from Jakarta meeting in possession of the author.

Hagiwara, Y. (1973). Formation and development of the Association of Southeast Asian Nations. *The Developing Economies* 11(4): 443-465.

Hall, C.M. (1994). *Tourism in the Pacific Rim: Development, Impacts and Markets*. Melbourne: Longman.

Hitchcock, M., King, V., and Parnwell, M. (1993). Tourism in South-East Asia: Introduction. In M. Hitchcock, V.T. King, and M.J.G. Parnwell (Eds.), *Tourism in South-East Asia* (pp. 1-31). London: Routledge.

Hoong, C.M. (1996). Bintan projects boost S'pore-Jakarta ties. *Straits Times,* June 19, p. 2.

Hussey, A. (1991). Regional development and cooperation through ASEAN. *Geographical Review* 81(1): 87-98.

Imada, P., Montes, M. and Naya, S. (1991). *A Free Trade Area: Implications for ASEAN*. Singapore: Institute of Southeast Asian Studies.

Jakarta Post (1998). Tourist arrivals up 5% in 1997. *The Jakarta Post,* June, 19.

Kamil, Y., Pangestu, M., and Fredericks, C. (1991). A Malaysian perspective. In L.T. Yuan (Ed.), *Growth Triangle: The Johor-Singapore-Riau Experience* (pp. 37-74). Singapore: Institute of Southeast Asian Studies.

Kliot, N. (1996). Turning desert to bloom: Israeli-Jordanian peace proposals for the Jordan Rift Valley. *Journal of Borderlands Studies* 11(1): 1-24.

Kumar, S. and Yuan, L.T. (1991). A Singapore perspective. In L.T. Yuan (Ed.), *Growth Triangle: The Johor-Singapore-Riau Experience* (pp. 2-36). Singapore: Institute of Southeast Asian Studies.

McCloud, D.G. (1995). *Southeast Asia: Tradition and Modernity in the Contemporary World.* Boulder, CO: Westview Press.

Milne, R.S. (1993). Singapore's growth triangle. *The Round Table* 327: 291-303.

Min, W.T. (1980). Growth of ASEAN trade and tourism. In S. Swee-Hock (Ed.), *ASEAN Economies in Transition* (pp. 243-294). Singapore: Singapore University Press.

Naidu, G. (1988). ASEAN cooperation in transport. In H. Esmara (Ed.), *ASEAN Economic Cooperation: A New Perspective* (pp. 191-204). Singapore: Chopmen Publishers.

Ooi, G.L. (1995). The Indonesia-Malaysia-Singapore growth triangle: Sub-regional economic cooperation and integration. *GeoJournal* 36(4): 337-344. Quoted material reprinted with kind permission from Kluwer Academic Publishers.

Pangestu, M. (1991). An Indonesian perspective. In L.T. Yuan (Ed.), *Growth Triangle: The Johor-Singapore-Riau Experience* (pp. 75-115). Singapore: Institute of Southeast Asian Studies.

Pangestu, M., Soesastro, H., and Ahmad, M. (1992). A new look at intra-ASEAN economic cooperation. *ASEAN Economic Bulletin* 8(3): 344-352.

Panitchapat, S. (1998). Keynote address. Presented at the Third International Conference on Tourism and Hotel Industry in Indochina and Southeast Asia. Phuket, Thailand, June 6.

Parsonage, J. (1992). Southeast Asia's "Growth Triangle": A subregional response to global transformation. *International Journal of Urban and Regional Research* 16(2): 307-317.

Perry, M. (1991). The Singapore growth triangle: State, capital and labour at a new frontier in the world economy. *Singapore Journal of Tropical Geography* 12(2): 138-151.

Radio Thailand (1995). Indonesia-Malaysia-Thailand growth triangle meeting. Radio Broadcast, Bangkok, December 19.

Ramos, F.V. (1995). Cross-border "growth triangles" promote prosperity in East Asia. *New Perspective Quarterly* 12(1): 12-13.

Richard, W.E. (1993). International planning for tourism. *Annals of Tourism Research* 20(4): 601-604.

Singapore Tourist Promotion Board/Bintan Resort Management Ltd. (n.d.), *Experience Singapore-Bintan, 2 Worlds, 45 Minutes Apart.* Singapore: STPB/ Bintan Resort Management Ltd./Indonesia Tourism Promotion Board.

Stockwin, H. (1975). ASEAN free trade gathers momentum. *Far Eastern Economic Review,* November 21, pp. 50-54.

Tasker, R., Schwarz, A., and Vatikiotis, M. (1994). ASEAN: Growing pains. *Far Eastern Economic Review,* July 28, pp. 22-23.

Timothy, D.J. (1995a). International boundaries: New frontiers for tourism research. *Progress in Tourism and Hospitality Research* 1(2): 141-152.

Timothy, D.J. (1995b). Political boundaries and tourism: Borders as tourist attractions. *Tourism Management* 16(7): 525-532.

Timothy, D.J. (1998). Cooperative tourism planning in a developing destination. *Journal of Sustainable Tourism* 6(1): 52-68.

Timothy, D.J. (1999). Cross-border cooperation in tourism resource management: A view of international parks along the US-Canada border. *Journal of Sustainable Tourism,* 7(2): 27-32.

Travel Indonesia (1991). ASEAN tourism growth. *Travel Indonesia,* March 7-8, pp. 27-28.

Travel Indonesia (1994). ASEAN tourism forum '94. *Travel Indonesia,* February 16-18, p. 31.

Tyler, C. (1992). Triangular bonds. *Geographical Magazine* 64(3): 34-37.

Wall, G. (1993). Toward a tourism typology. In J.G. Nelson, R.W. Butler, and G. Wall (Eds.), *Tourism and Sustainable Development: Monitoring, Planning, Managing* (pp. 45-58). Waterloo, ON: Department of Geography, University of Waterloo.

Walton, J. (1993). Tourism and economic development in ASEAN. In M. Hitchcock, V.T. King, and M.J.G. Parnwell (Eds.), *Tourism in South-East Asia* (pp. 214-233). London: Routledge.

Wee, A. (1996). Bintan resort to have 3,000 hotel rooms by year 2000. *Business Times,* June 19, p. 4.

Wichaidit, T. (1998). Keynote address. Presented at the Third International Conference on Tourism and Hotel Industry in Indochina and Southeast Asia. Phuket, Thailand, June 5.

Wong, D. (1996). Two new investors to give $300m boost to Bintan resorts. *Straits Times,* June 19, p. 2.

Wong, J. (1989). The ASEAN model of regional cooperation. In S. Naya, M. Urrutia, S. Mark, and A. Fuentes (Eds.), *Lessons in Development: A Comparative Study of Asia and Latin America* (pp. 121-141). San Francisco: International Center for Economic Growth.

Wong, S.C.M. (1987). ASEAN co-operation in tourism: Looking back and looking forward. In C.L. Lee and L.L. Jin (Eds.), *ASEAN at the Crossroads* (pp. 371-393). Kuala Lumpur: Institute of Strategic and International Studies.

Chapter 3

Ecotourism and Sustainable Tourism Development in Southeast Asia

John Edmonds
George Leposky

INTRODUCTION

Would the goal of environmental preservation be better served if wildlife and wilderness were placed off-limits to holidaymakers? That's the view of Richard Leakey (1998), paleontologist and director of the National Museum of Kenya. He believes that ecotourism has become a label prone to abuse, fostering incursions into "areas of enormous biological importance that cannot sustain utilization by large numbers of people." Such areas, he says, would be better off if holidaymakers watched nature on TV instead of going to visit it.

We respectfully disagree. In our view, preservation of ecologically sensitive areas and visitation of such areas by holidaymakers need not be mutually exclusive. Indeed, visitation in such areas can broaden awareness of their existence and unique characteristics, and help to build a constituency dedicated to their protection and preservation.

As French (1998) notes, "Ecotourism is [a] possible vehicle for channeling international investment capital into the preservation of threatened ecosystems, if it is pursued in an ecologically sensitive manner. . . . Since ecotourism is not generally capital-intensive, domestic investment may often be sufficient for underwriting much of the industry. But even ecotourism has its infrastructure: international investment may find a role in upgrading airports and building the kind of carefully conceived, small-scale, low-impact hotels that are consistent with the industry's conservation goals" (p. 25).

To illustrate this proposition, we present a case study from the state of Sarawak, Malaysia, where the state government has taken an active role in the development of tourism infrastructure, including properties with strong ecotouristic aspects.

The Sarawak experience also demonstrates that the form of hospitality accommodation known variously around the world as timesharing, interval ownership, holiday ownership, and vacation ownership constitutes a viable adjunct to the development of a sustainable tourism industry based on ecotourism.

DEFINITIONS

The concept of ecotourism arises from the science called ecology (study of the interrelationships among organisms and their environment), a word based upon the Greek *oikos* (house) and *logos* (word). Because *Homo sapiens* is an organism interacting with the environment like any other, ecology entails respect for indigenous human cultures as well as the preservation of natural biological communities. Ecotourism, then, ideally refers to visitation methods that minimize disruption of the host locale's distinctive attributes.

In defining sustainable tourism development, Moore (1996) begins with the World Tourism Organization's characterization—that to be sustainable, tourism development must meet the needs of present tourists and host regions while protecting and enhancing opportunities for the future. Then he goes on to define the concept more broadly, speaking in terms of "total integration with the community in which you are [located]."

Total integration involves consideration of health and safety aspects, conservation of natural resources, renewable energy supplies, and other environmental manifestations. In addition, total integration involves maintaining the lifestyle and dignity of indigenous inhabitants by protecting the social fabric of the local community, assuring local economic opportunities, and guarding against exploitation by the outside world (Leposky, 1997).

Writing of sustainable development in general, Goldmark (1995) includes in his "characteristics of the new path" more effective accounting systems to calculate the costs and benefits of resource-utilization strategies, ready availability of family planning and reproductive health services, more emphasis on quality-of-life issues, and "concepts of equity more related to educational opportunity and less concerned with material goods" (p. 6).

Simons and Leposky (1994) define a timeshare project as "a project in which a purchaser receives the right in perpetuity for life or for a term of years to the recurrent exclusive use or occupancy of a lot, parcel unit, or segment of real property annually or on some other periodic basis. Such a timeshare project covers a specified period of time allotted from the use or occupancy periods into which the project has been divided" (p. 119). In Southeast Asia, most timeshare projects are structured on a right-to-use basis spanning a period of years, throughout which the developer remains in control of the property. For a project designed to foster ecotourism and sustainability, this ownership arrangement provides continuity in management of the resort to assure ongoing adherence to the original objectives.

Purchasers of timeshares are not restricted to holidaymaking at the resort where they own timeshares. Two global timeshare-exchange networks exist: Interval International, based in Miami, Florida; and Resort Condominiums International, based in Indianapolis, Indiana. The vast majority of timeshare resorts are affiliated with one or the other.

Holiday owners at an ecotouristic resort may, on occasion, wish to exchange elsewhere for a different kind of holiday experience. In so doing, they create exchange inventory that can be used by people who own timeshares elsewhere and want to exchange into a resort offering an ecologically oriented holiday. (Also, until the resort is sold out, vacant developer-owned inventory will be available for inward exchange.)

THE SARAWAK EXPERIENCE

Rugged mountains shrouded in mist, massive cave systems still largely unexplored, and spectacular waterfalls set in a verdant rainforest of incredible beauty and diversity attract visitors from all over the world to the interior of Borneo, the world's third largest island (Robles-Espinoza, 1996). To build a viable tourism industry around the natural attributes of this wild, remote region, the Sarawak state government in Malaysia has committed substantial resources through its development arm, the Sarawak Economic Development Corporation (SEDC).

SEDC views tourism and leisure as a "strategic business unit" equal in stature to roads and works, food-based industries, agro-based industries, mineral and mining/building materials, human resource development (e.g., education), and Bumiputra (indigenous peoples) commercial and industrial community-development programs.

In the tourism and leisure sector, SEDC has invested over 550 million Malaysian ringgits—equivalent to approximately US$154,275,000 at the March 27, 1998, New York foreign exchange selling rate (Currency Trading, 1998)—to build five "international standard" hotels and other tourism properties, plus downtown shopping complexes in Sarawak's capital city, Kuching; the Damai Golf and Country Club; and the Sarawak Cultural Village (*S.E.D.C. Sarawak*, n.d.). The cultural village—a seventeen-acre (6.9-hectare) tourist attraction twenty-two miles (35 kilometers) from Kuching in the Damai Beach resort district—is a "living museum" that enables visitors to experience in half a day the authentic dwelling styles, arts, crafts, games, foods, music, and dance of seven of Sarawak's major resident cultures (*Sarawak Cultural Village*, n.d.).

Two of the SEDC resorts, Bukit Saban and Royal Mulu, are located deep within Borneo's interior rainforest and serve as a comfortable base for ecotouristic adventures. Camp Permai, in the Damai Beach resort district, offers a more accessible ecotourism experience in a naturalistic setting.

Bukit Saban is a fifty-unit resort built in 1995 on a fourteen-acre (5.7-hectare) site in the Paku district of Betong, 180 miles (290 kilometers) from Kuching. The buildings that house its accommodations resemble the apartment-style longhouses of the Iban tribe (Leposky, 1996b).

In the vicinity of the resort are actual Iban villages where the inhabitants welcome Bukit Saban Resort guests and timeshare owners and share such aspects of the indigenous culture as cockfighting matches, traditional dances, arts and crafts, and cuisine. Bukit Saban Resort also offers guided bicycle, boat, and foot trips in the surrounding terrain. Destinations include nearby cocoa, oil-palm, and pepper plantations, and a waterfall in the jungle reached by a trek through rugged terrain. Additionally, within twelve miles (twenty kilometers) of the resort, guests and timeshare owners may visit a government agricultural research center devoted to the farming of freshwater fish and to cultivation of wild fruits, ferns, and durian and rubber trees (Leposky, 1996a).

Royal Mulu Resort was built in 1992 on a 200-acre (81-hectare) site along the Melinau River adjoining Gunung Mulu National Park, six to seven hours upriver by boat from the coast of the South China Sea. Malaysia Airlines transports most of the resort's supplies and visitors to a small local airport from Miri, the nearest city, on forty-five-minute flights aboard a nineteen-seat Twin Otter aircraft. The resort's accommodations consist of 149 units in longhouse-style structures resembling the architecture of a nearby Penan tribal village, connected by boardwalks. The entire resort is built on stilts more than thirty feet (nine meters) above the ground, well above the high-water mark of the adjacent river's recurrent floods. A net-draped walk-through aviary on the resort grounds harbors a representative assortment of native birds, including the state bird of Sarawak, the hornbill (Leposky, 1996b).

The vast Gunung Mulu National Park encompasses 210 square miles (544 square kilometers) of mountainous rainforest bisected by rivers and streams. Recreational activities in the national park include scaling three major mountains, Mulu (7,796 feet/2,376 meters), Api (5,611 feet/1,710 meters), and Benarat (5,200 feet/1,585 meters); climbing to a rain-sculpted rock formation called The Pinnacles on Mt. Api; canoeing and rafting on the Melinau River; and exploring the world's largest limestone cave system, in which more than 125 miles (200 kilometers) of passages have been surveyed and twice or thrice that length remain to be explored (Kumar, 1996; Reed, 1996).

Park officials have established four "show caves"—Clearwater, Wind, Deer, and Lang. Arrangements may be made at Royal Mulu Resort to visit them, accompanied by guides from the nearby Orang Ulu tribe.

Deer Cave is the world's largest known underground chamber, 394 feet (120 meters) high and 328 feet (100 meters) wide. Clear-water Cave is the longest cave passage in Asia and the seventh longest known in the world, extending at least sixty-six miles (107 kilo-meters). Wind and Lang caves, though smaller, are renowned for the superlative quality of their rock formations.

Clearwater and Wind caves may be reached aboard motorized longboats traveling upriver from the resort, and all four caves also are accessible by means of boardwalks from the park headquarters. Besides easing the way of visitors over uneven terrain, these well-defined pathways help to protect the surrounding jungle. By the same token, well-lit concrete paths and stairways facilitate touristic visitation within these caves, while minimizing the impact of human presence upon the caves' rock formations and the various animal and plant species residing within (Leposky, 1996a; *National Parks*, n.d.; Reed, 1996).

For adventure cavers who seek to explore beyond the beaten path, application for permission may be made in advance to the national park. With the assistance of park officials, Reed (1996) has compiled a list of at least eighteen separate routes through the cave system, ranging in length from 2,900 feet (885 meters) to 15.5 miles (25 kilometers). Many of these expeditions require knowledge of technical rope work for rappelling and climbing.

Camp Permai consists of twenty-nine cabins and ten treehouses on a forty-four-acre (17.8-hectare) site on a forested slope beside the South China Sea. The camp includes an outdoor activity center where skilled instructors teach survival skills, including the use of ropes as an aid to movement, and knowledge of edible jungle fruits and plants. Conferencing facilities are available. For families, students, and corporate groups, the camp offers programs designed to build individual self-confidence and interpersonal interaction skills (*Camp Permai Outdoor Activity Centre*, n.d.).

THE ROLE OF HOLIDAY OWNERSHIP

In 1995, SEDC allocated 30 percent of its hotel and resort industry to timesharing, and established a subsidiary, Asia Vacations Club Sdn. Bhd., doing business as Club Asia International, to sell timeshare packages. Sales began in 1996, and as of 1998 Club Asia International had close to 500 members—a respectable showing in view of the fact that most Sarawakians have never before been exposed to the timeshare concept.

After some administrative difficulties that led to a reorganization and a five-month hiatus in active sales, Club Asia International relaunched its sales effort in February 1998. A sales force numbering about thirty now operates from a sales center in the Sarawak Shopping Mall in downtown Kuching. Another office was opened in Kuala Lumpur later in 1998.

The Club Asia program is based upon the sale of points, which club members can use in a variety of ways during the twenty-five-year term of their membership. Possibilities include accommodations at six SEDC-owned hotels and resorts in Sarawak, including Bukit Saban and Royal Mulu resorts and Camp Permai; amenities, recreational activities, sightseeing adventures, and travel; and exchange opportunities through the worldwide auspices of Interval International's exchange network, known in North America as the Quality Vacation Exchange Network and in Europe and Asia as the Quality Holiday Exchange Network (*Club Asia,* n.d.; Leposky, 1996b).

The Interval International exchange network encompasses nearly 1,600 resorts in more than eighty countries around the world, at which some 860,000 consumer members own timeshares (Interval International Fact Sheet, 1998). To use their exchange privileges with Interval, Club Asia members may submit enough points to Club Asia to secure a week's accommodations at one of its properties, then relinquish those accommodations to the Interval network and select accommodations of comparable value and quality from Interval's inventory.

In turn, the Club Asia weeks in the Interval network become available for use by Interval members who own elsewhere and have relinquished their home-resort accommodations in return for an exchange.

CONCLUSION

We have demonstrated the value of ecotourism as a focal point for sustainable tourism development, using as an illustration the experience of the state of Sarawak, Malaysia; and we have shown the role that holiday ownership plays in that experience.

Holiday ownership adds value to a sustainable ecotouristic enterprise in two ways. First, it creates a reservoir of owner-members who have made a commitment to the project. By virtue of that commitment, they are likely to return with greater frequency than the average transient guest. This is one reason why timeshare resorts and mixed-use (hotel and holiday ownership) properties tend to have higher occupancy than most hotels without a holiday ownership component. Moreover, when holiday owners exchange away from their home resort, they create an exchange-network inventory that someone else is likely to use to exchange in, thus maintaining the home resort's occupancy rate—and the level of revenues generated by food and beverage outlets, guide services, boat and bicycle rental, and other fee-based amenities and activities.

Timeshare exchange also has the potential to attract timeshare visitors from all parts of the world to ecotouristic resorts. The comparability aspect of the exchange process makes it especially attractive to travelers from distant locations. They can be assured that, no matter how wild and remote the destination, the accommodations awaiting them will meet the same standards of comfort and overall quality they selected at the home resort where they purchased their own timeshare.

REFERENCES

Camp Permai Outdoor Activity Centre (n.d.). Brochure. Pantai Damai, Santubong, Sarawak: Camp Permai Outdoor Activity Centre.

Club Asia International Overview (n.d.). Report. Kuching, Sarawak: Asia Vacations Club Sdn. Bhd.

Currency trading (1998). *The Wall Street Journal,* March 30, c. 18.

French, H.F. (1998). *Investing in the Future: Harnessing Private Capital Flows for Environmentally Sustainable Development.* Washington, DC: Worldwatch Institute.

Goldmark, P.C., Jr. (1995). The president's letter. *The Rockefeller Foundation 1994 Annual Report.* New York: The Rockefeller Foundation.

Interval International Fact Sheet (1998). Corporate document. Miami: Interval International, Inc.

Kumar, G.S. (1996). *Visitors' Guide to Malaysia.* Kuala Lumpur, Malaysia: Tourism Publications Corporation Sdn. Bhd.

Leakey, R. (1998). Address. Florida International University. Miami, Florida.

Leposky, G. (1996a). Ecotourism: "Spreading the word about the house." *Vacation Industry Review,* November/December: 44-47.

Leposky, G. (1996b). State-owned company in Sarawak launches a vacation club. *Vacation Industry Review,* November/December: 38-41.

Leposky, G. (1997). Globalization and sustainable development. *Vacation Industry Review,* March/April: 10.

Moore, W. (1996). Address. Miami Conference on the Caribbean and Latin America. Miami, Florida.

National Parks, Nature Reserves, and Wildlife Centres of Sarawak (n.d.). Brochure. Sarawak: National Parks and Wildlife Section, Forest Department.

Reed, M. (1996). Gunung Mulu National Park. Unpublished manuscript.

Robles-Espinoza, J.C. (1996). *Sarawak.* Brochure. Kuching, Sarawak: Sarawak Tourism Board.

Sarawak Cultural Village (n.d.). Brochure.

S.E.D.C. Sarawak (n.d.). Annual report.

Simons, A.H. and Leposky, G. (1994). *AEI Resource Manual.* Washington, DC: American Resort Development Association.

Chapter 4

Dreams and Realities: Vulnerability and the Tourism Industry in Southeast Asia: A Framework for Analyzing and Adapting Tourism Management Toward 2000

Alan Nankervis

INTRODUCTION

Recent currency crises in many Southeast Asian nations (e.g., Thailand, Malaysia, Indonesia), perceptions of social or political instability (e.g., Myanmar, Cambodia), ideological differences (e.g., Vietnam, People's Republic of China), and even smog levels (e.g., forest fires in Sumatra and Kalimantan in 1997) inevitably have repercussions for regional tourism industries.

These effects may not always be adverse—currency fluctuations, for example, may actually enhance inbound tourism from less affected regions (*The Australian,* 1997a; *Travel Week,* 1997; *Australian Financial Review,* 1997d); perceptions of political instability in countries such as Myanmar and Cambodia may benefit more stable destinations such as Malaysia, Singapore, or Australia; active promotional campaigns such as the recent "Amazing Thailand" campaign (Tourism Authority of Thailand, 1998; *Asian Business Review,* 1998) may attract foreign currency to redress the causes of the initial problem. Conversely, Australia's tourism trade from Southeast Asian nations has been reduced as a consequence of unfavorable currency exchange rates (*Australian Financial Review,* 1997c; *Courier Mail,*

1997; *Sydney Morning Herald,* 1997a; *West Australian,* 1997b), and to a lesser extent, due to perceptions of physical danger in some locations (e.g., Gold Coast, King's Cross) and the "Pauline Hanson factor" (*Herald Sun,* 1996a, 1996b). Singapore's tourism potential has been lessened by perceptions that it is less exciting than neighboring destinations. Despite admirable promotional efforts, Sentosa Island remains less attractive than Bali, Penang, Phuket, or Pattaya.

Such pressures on the tourism industry may be either short term or enduring, but they are seldom linear or simple. More often than not they result from extremely complex relationships between a host of global, regional, local, and industry variables, which contain both controllable and seemingly uncontrollable factors threatening even the best-laid strategies and plans of government, industry, and individual tourist agency managers. In essence, they highlight the inherent fragility and complexity of this increasingly crucial sector of all regional economies (Go and Jenkins, 1997; Griffin and Darcy, 1997).

This chapter presents work in progress toward an analytical framework incorporating many of the variables that characterize the tourism industry in all regional countries, and which almost inherently predispose it to *vulnerability* (*Business Review Weekly,* 1988; *Australian Financial Review,* 1993). This framework encompasses both external and internal industry factors, and suggests strategies that can be adopted to protect and to buffer the industry from the most severe impacts of these pressures. The "vulnerability framework" is derived from a variety of conceptual and empirical sources. Conceptually, its origins lie in contingency, systems, chaos, and crisis management theories. It is empirically based on the limited amount of research on tourism management, both globally and within the region. Potential applications of this framework, when fully developed both as an analytical tool and as development methodology for tourism, are broad, but for the purposes of this chapter will be restricted to three disparate elements—currency crises, airplane disasters, and the relationships between tourism and hospitality.

NATURE OF THE TOURISM INDUSTRY

The tourism and hospitality industry, almost by definition, is characterized by a unique degree of vulnerability at all levels of its operations (Griffin and Darcy, 1997; Hall, 1994). Considering vulnerability as the broad exposure to risk, the industry is inherently sensitive to international, regional, and national pressures and susceptible to the impact of political, socioeconomic, and market developments. Ironically, even as it grows in size and economic importance, risk exposure increases rather than decreases.

Some, or all, of these risk factors increase the vulnerability of some, or all, levels of the industry either predictably or unpredictably (the "butterfly effect" of chaos theory). As examples, the recent smoke haze over much of Southeast Asia has, together with the currency crisis, perhaps both enhanced and threatened tourism in Thailand, Malaysia, and Indonesia, inbound or outbound (*Australian Financial Review*, 1997a). Similarly, the incorporation of Hong Kong into the People's Republic of China (PRC) has apparently adversely affected tourism in Hong Kong but not the PRC (*Asian Business Review*, 1998).

Vulnerability can be experienced at the *industry* (macro) level, the *interface* (mosaic) level, the individual agency or *organizational* (micro) level, or at all three levels. "Interface" here refers to the often problematic linkages between industry sectors (e.g., between travel agents, immigration officials, airline operators, hotels, and tour operators). As an example, a first time traveler to Phuket may experience a series of unfortunate *interface incidents* such as slow check-in procedures, delayed flights, lost luggage, abusive customs officials, health problems, or unfriendly hotel staff, which predispose them against a repeat visit. The converse is hopefully (more often than not) also true, but the disparate and disconnected nature of tourism service providers cannot easily ensure this.

Risks are aggravated at all levels by the nontangible qualities of the "product" (Zeithaml, Parasuraman, and Berry, 1990), and the "mosaic" (or "jigsaw") rather than linear, configuration of its internal linkages. Thus, just as every service encounter is unique, so are the links between a series of such encounters (i.e., a holiday or a business trip involving reservations, travel, accommodation, tours, and dining), and each stage is "managed" by a series of unrelated service providers.

AN ANALYTICAL AND DEVELOPMENTAL
FRAMEWORK FOR VULNERABILITY
IN THE TOURISM INDUSTRY

Figure 4.1 encapsulates our thoughts toward a framework that will assist managers in the tourism industry to analyze potential (and actual) macro- and microthreats to their profitability and long-term survival prospects, and implies strategies that they may choose to adopt.

The horizontal axis encompasses the range of macroissues which continually provide either threats or opportunities (and sometimes both) to the entire tourism industry or its component parts and regions. Thus vulnerability may be exacerbated or reduced by such factors as:

- International, regional, and national *political* issues (e.g., level of security and stability, government priorities and funding, ideological factors)
- Global and domestic *economic* issues (e.g., currency fluctuations, comparative buying power of consumer markets)
- *Social* and *cross-cultural* issues (e.g., preferences for domestic and/or international tourism, xenophobic attitudes, religious priorities)
- *Guest market* issues (e.g., leisure/business travel, packaged tours versus backpacking, ecotourism, and adventure travel)
- *Tourism product* issues (e.g., new versus old locations or properties, service quality—pricing aspects, reliability and consistency factors)
- *Industry structural* issues (e.g., relationships between tourism and hospitality segments, public versus private providers, strategic global and domestic operator alliances)
- *Geographic locational* issues (e.g., relative attractiveness, tourism infrastructure, images)
- *Physical* issues (e.g., new versus old properties, ease of travel, guest security, terrorism threats)

Most destinations and their tourism providers will be affected by some or all of these factors, often on ongoing bases. As examples, Singapore as a tourist destination is perceived as a politically stable, economically secure, and relatively safe environment. Jakarta, on the

FIGURE 4.1. An Analytical Framework for Vulnerability in the Tourism Industry

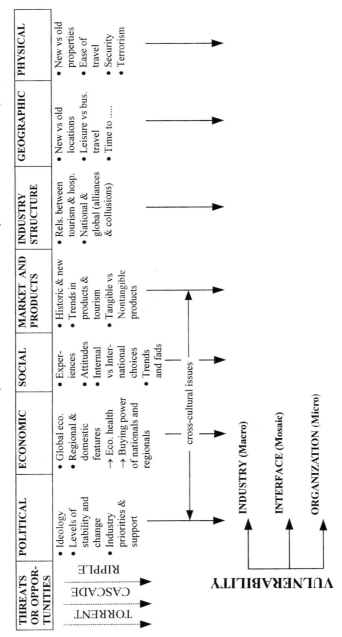

53

other hand, has been perceived as less politically and economically stable but with more long-term business possibilities and with access to a broader range of opportunities in Java and Sumatra. Sydney possesses relative political and economic stability and a broad range of add-on tourist facilities but with less "exotic" Asian characteristics.

Whereas the horizontal axis of the framework illustrates the range of potential threats to the industry, the vertical axis reflects the depth of the impact of each variable on the discrete levels of the tourism industry—e.g., industry, interface, and individual organization.

The calculation of the potential impacts of macroissues on the separate levels of the tourism industry also involves some evaluation of the degree of their immediate and long-term effects, and should properly be built into strategic planning at all levels. These effects are included in the framework as "ripple," "cascade," and "torrent" effects. Ripple effects generally affect several sectors, or regions of the industry but minimally and only in the short term. Cascade effects usually have an impact over more sectors or regions and can last longer, while torrent effects can have substantial and long-term consequences. As examples, the resumption of Hong Kong by the People's Republic of China in July 1997 appears to have had an adverse ripple effect on air travel and hotel bookings in Hong Kong (*Asian Business Review*, 1998); smog levels from Sumatran fires may have had a cascade effect on all tourism sectors in all surrounding countries (*The Australian*, 1997b; *Australian Financial Review*, 1997a); a series of air disasters in different parts of the world will undoubtedly have a torrent effect on all sectors of tourism throughout the world. The following three case examples illustrate the analytical features of this chapter's framework (see Figure 4.1) in relation to: *Economic Structure, Physical Structure,* and *Industry Structure.*

CASE 1: CURRENCY CRISES
AND TOURISM IN SOUTHEAST ASIA

Tourism in Southeast Asia has historically attracted travelers from outside the region, between and within regional countries, and itinerant commuters on the "Kangaroo route" from Australia and New Zealand bound for the United States, United Kingdom, and Europe (and vice versa). A mixture of business and leisure guests, backpackers, honeymooners, would-be joint venturers, expatriates, nervous university students, and retired, wealthy tourists have frequented the numerous five-star hotels, guesthouses, and youth hostels spread from Bali and Jakarta, to Singapore, Kuala Lumpur, Penang, Phuket, Pattaya, Bangkok, and to more "adventurous" locations such as Myanmar, Cambodia, Laos, Vietnam, and the People's Republic of China. The comparative safety, "internationalism" of facilities and associated infrastructure, competitive pricing, and breadth of add-on tourist sights in all Southeast Asian countries have ensured repeat guest business and the consequent centrality of tourism to national economic prosperity (Go and Jenkins, 1997; Griffin and Darcy, 1997).

A significant attractor to increasing tourism in Southeast Asian destinations in recent years has been the favorable currency exchange rates for visitors from the United States, the United Kingdom, Europe, and Australia. In addition, sunny climates, friendly and attentive hotel employees, the prospect of "exotic" locations, and "bargains" (e.g., clothing, food, electronic goods, etc.) have provided powerful incentives for visitors to locations such as Bali, Kuala Lumpur, Pattaya, Penang, Phuket, and Bangkok. The perceived political stability of most of these countries, together with their relative physical security, has assured tourists of the attractiveness of these destinations. With differentiated but regular guest markets, both resort and capital city locations in Southeast Asia have benefited from these characteristics (Seow, Tucker, and Sundberg, 1984).

In late 1997 and early 1998, however, guest perceptions have begun to change, with the association of currency and sociopolitical instabilities. While the depreciation of the Thai and Indonesian currencies should have increased the levels of tourism within those countries and their tourist destinations, especially for nonregional inbound tourism, the associated concerns about political and social instability may have simultaneously deterred nervous tourists and business travelers (*Australian Financial Review,* 1997b, 1997e; *Sydney Morning Herald,* 1997b).

Broad economic pressures on the various governments in the region have provoked diverse responses in relation to the tourism industry. Thus the Thai government has proactively sought to attract more inbound tourism, and thence more foreign currency, both within and outside Southeast Asia, with its "Amazing Thailand" (TAT, 1998) promotional campaign. Both Malaysia and Indonesia have focused on restricting overseas outbound tourism. Dr. Mahathir, for example, has urged Malaysians to stay home (Tourism Authority of Thailand, 1998), and Indonesia has launched a "love the rupiah" campaign and provided limits on the amount of currency that can be taken outside the country. Anecdotally, all three countries, far from reducing holiday or business traveler costs to induce tourist spending, have either increased local prices for visitors and/or quoted costs in U.S. dollars in order to recover some financial advantage.

Arguably, both inbound and outbound tourism provide significant financial returns to local providers, including income for airlines, governments, travel agencies, and hoteliers in their various destinations. In Indonesia, for example, specified tourism taxes (e.g., 2 percent taxes on hotel accommodation as a tourism surcharge) and a departure levy for outbound locals (US$150) have for some time provided a valuable return to government agencies, both subsidizing associated costs and adding to overall revenue. Disincentives to travel from Indonesia, without associated incentives (as in Thailand) for inbound tourism only serve to diminish the overall contribution of the industry to its faltering economy. At this time of unstable regional currencies, tourism may provide one of the means by which financial stability can be assisted. Given the centrality of tourism to many regional economies, now should be the time for proactive economic policies to redress downturns (Tourism Authority of Thailand, 1998; Go and Jenkins, 1997).

For the hospitality sector, in particular, disincentives to inbound tourism provide substantial threats for individual hoteliers, resort operators, or even entire regions. Disincentives for outbound business or leisure travel from Southeast Asia also have significant short- and long-term effects on the profitability of Australian and New Zealand hotels. If joint venture opportunities between Southeast Asia and Australia are to recede as a consequence of fluctuating exchange rates, then both geographic regions will suffer, within the context of the global economy (Griffin and Darcy, 1997).

Already, Australian tourism authorities (e.g., Tourism Task Force, Tourism Council of Australia) predicted substantially reduced levels of tourism (and thence hotel occupancy) to Australia from Southeast Asian nations stretching to the Olympic Games in 2000 (*West Australian,* 1997a; *Australian Financial Review,* 1997b, 1997e). In the immediate term, the Commonwealth Games in Kuala Lumpur in 1998 were considered adversely affected. On the other hand, supportive government policies such as those implemented in Thailand may prove effective in reversing this negative trend. In an already competitive regional tourism industry, Thailand may be the "winner" as a consequence of the more proactive policies adopted by its government (Tourism Authority of Thailand, 1998).

In relation to the proposed framework of vulnerability, Thailand's relative political stability (less than Malaysia, but more than Indonesia) may be the determining factor for enhancing tourism to its discrete destinations. At this time of uncertainty, the prime imperative of hoteliers should be to emphasize the security, relative economy, and unique attractions of their locations and properties, and to optimize their comparative advantages against their competitors. As examples, hoteliers could focus on their traditional target markets (e.g., older, wealthier, and longer-term guests in Penang, Phuket, and Sanur; younger, short-term travelers to Bali and Pattaya; business visitors to Singapore, Bangkok, and Sydney) and maximize their comparative regional advantages (e.g., political stability in Thailand, Malaysia, Singapore, and Sydney).

The currency crisis can be characterized as a short-term cascade (rather than a longer term torrent) effect with significant advantages for inbound tourism, provided that all hotel guests are assured of their personal safety, enjoyment, and satisfaction within defined parameters well-communicated to travel agencies, government authorities, and tourism operators. In this way, the perceptions of their diverse guest markets may be reassured and the continuing returns of hoteliers guaranteed. If these outcomes cannot be achieved, the tourism industries of Southeast Asian nations will inevitably suffer from the adverse perceptions of their potential guests.

Some regional countries (e.g., Malaysia, Thailand, Singapore, Australia) are better positioned than others (e.g., Indonesia, Myanmar, Cambodia) to benefit from these endeavors, but all tourism industries (and their component parts) will need to develop appropriate strategies that will enable them to overcome, and profit from, the opportunities and disadvantages offered by such currency exchange rate fluctuations. If they fail to do so, it will be the result of short-sighted government policies, inappropriate industry strategies, or unresponsive hospitality managers (Go and Jenkins, 1997; Griffin and Darcy, 1997).

CASE 2: AIRPLANE DISASTERS AND TOURISM IMPACTS

While it can be argued that currency fluctuations have a short-term cascade effect on all components of the tourism industry, and that some (at least) of these effects can be beneficial to the countries involved, the impact of airplane disasters are more long-lasting, and combined with other factors (e.g., political instability, social problems, physical security issues) can create torrent impacts on the entire tourism industries of the concerned countries.

As examples, the two domestic airline disasters that occurred in Indonesia during 1997 (Garuda Indonesia crashes in Java and Sumatra) and the single Silk Air crash in Sumatra have arguably affected the tourism industries of Indonesia and Singapore in different ways.

Although the Garuda disasters were domestic, and the Silk Air crash international, the impacts on tourism have been both similar and different. Usher (1997, p. 56) suggests that: ". . . the terror of cruising through the clouds one moment and nose diving earthwards the next is as primordial and petrifying as the nightmare of [a shark's] dorsal fins and triangular teeth." However, passenger perceptions of the relative safety of regional airlines and their destinations' security and attractiveness plays a large part in their choice of subsequent locations and carriers.

Thus Garuda Indonesia (international) has a relatively unblemished record in the last decade, while Silk Air is a new international/ regional carrier. Garuda is, however, associated (in potential travelers' minds) with the sociopolitical unrest in Indonesia, recent smoke haze problems, and the comparatively less attractive tourist destinations in Java and Sumatra. Silk Air, by contrast, is closely associated in travelers' minds with its parent company (Singapore Airlines), and with the political stability, orderliness, and efficiency of the Singaporean state. Singapore is also perceived by international travelers as the hub of Southeast Asia, which Singapore Airlines and Silk Air services.

Of consequence here also is the proliferation of alternative airline's that serve the different regions in which both Garuda Indonesia and Silk Air operate. For example, Bali and, to a lesser extent, Lombok are the destinations of choice for Australian, regional, and European tourists. Quantas and Ansett airlines (Australian) compete vigorously with Garuda Indonesia on these routes, but no such similar competition is experienced by Silk Air in its esoteric regional routes—e.g., Phuket, Jakarta, Penang.

Accordingly, it is perhaps not too surprising that the effects on Garuda Indonesia and Silk Air, as a consequence of their recent airline disasters, have been quite diverse. Garuda has experienced a dramatic reduction in traveler demand while Silk Air (and Singapore Airlines) have experienced only a short-term decline.

In these cases, it may have been more useful for both airlines (and their governments) to emphasize their previous good safety records, to reduce travel charges, or to provide attractive and competitive tourism packages emphasizing both the comparative advantages of their airlines and the exotic features of their destinations. Neither airline has so far capitalized on these features nor promoted the advantages of flying with these airlines (Rosenthal, t'Hart, and Kouzmin, 1991; Rosenthal and Kouzmin, 1993).

CASE 3: TOURISM AND HOSPITALITY— A FRAGMENTED INDUSTRY

Unlike the two previous examples, this case study illuminates the inherent fragmentation and segregation of the tourism industry, and illustrates the impact of vulnerability on all of its sectors. It can be empirically demonstrated and will subsequently be, but in this chapter it is based upon a theoretical analysis of the problematic interfaces between its disparate elements.

As earlier implied, the tourism industries of all countries in the region (and globally) are characterized by interdependence between nations, and between sectors of the industry. Thus inbound tourism to Thailand or Malaysia may be associated with leisure and/or business tourism to Singapore, Australia, the United States, or Europe. Such tours inevitably combine travel arrangements with hotel bookings, restaurant visits, and/or associated business and leisure packages. Almost all such combinations will involve the merging of public and private sector tourism agencies (e.g., immigration/customs officials, taxi and coach services, hospitality institutions, travel agents, and regional airlines) within a fragmented but apparently integrated system of tourism service delivery. Both public and private sector agencies may *attempt* to provide the optimum service quality (Zeithaml, Parasuraman, and Berry, 1990) in their discrete contributions to the tourism product—integrated by the responsible government coordinating and promotional campaigns—but few of the relevant actors in this process can *guarantee* the maintenance of consistent customer orientation (Heskett, Sasser, and Hart, 1990) and quality across the various tourism components that constitute the industry in any regional country (or across diverse nations).

The multiple interfaces between the travel agents' best-laid plans; the relative efficiency of travel and tourism operators; the equity or friendliness of immigration or customs officials; the timeliness and safety of airlines; and the service quality of hospitality institutions will affect (positively or negatively) the experiences of erstwhile tourism clients. Even in the relatively simple first overseas visit of a tourist from Japan to Australia, the perceptions and actual experiences of this interface may be crucial.

As an illustrative example, the naive tourist leaves Japan, singly or as part of a group tour, having planned for a pleasurable and safe one-week visit to Bali, Sydney, and Cairns. His (or her) experience includes a pleasant and efficient flight to Denpasar, some hassles from suspicious immigration officials, and a mild case of gastroenteritis in Bali, but overall a friendly reception among the shopkeepers and restauranteurs, and, subsequently, a robbery in Sydney and a delayed return flight to Japan. Will this tourist recommend Bali or Sydney to his or her friends and relatives in Japan? What can the tourism industry in either country do to redress (potential) negative perceptions? Will they even be aware of these issues?

The issue here is that the complex interfaces between the diverse (and often dissociated) sectors of tourism are often acknowledged, but seldom effectively addressed, to the detriment of the industry as a whole. In the case of tourism industries between disparate countries, these issues are almost never confronted. Although such anecdotal examples are seldom perceived as crises, given the importance of word-of-mouth marketing within the industry (and the fragmentation of the promotional campaigns of diverse industry sectors), the problematic interface between tourism industry components assumes major importance, in both the short and longer term. The vulnerability impact here may be categorized as a ripple, cascade, or (possibly) a torrent effect, depending on the degree of perceived (or actual) impact. Crisis management theory (Rosenthal and Kouzmin, 1993) implies both short-term solutions, and longer-term strategies, based upon clear identification of the relevant linkages and practical techniques for the amelioration of such interface issues. Will the tourism industries of regional countries be so adaptable?

CONCLUSION

The preceding three case examples are presented as illustrations of the (potential) applications of the analytical framework of vulnerability in the tourism industry. Although different in nature, each case example reflects common issues that require attention by industry associations, governments, individual tourism and hospitality operators, or preferably a combination of these.

Crisis management theory (Rosenthal, t'Hart, and Kouzmin, 1991; Rosenthal and Kouzmin, 1993) suggests that each case demands both short-term and more strategic responses—"in many crises, there will be a need to explore long-term consequences even though the situation at hand may seem to ask exclusively for immediate short-term action" (Rosenthal and Kouzmin, 1993, p. 5). Thus, in the case of currency crises, long-term solutions (e.g., government and international economic strategies, restructuring of banking and finance systems), as well as shorter-term tourism initiatives (e.g., promotional campaigns, reduced travel and hotel pricing) may assist the resolution of the problem.

In the case of airline disasters, both strategies will be required to reinforce the safety and cost-benefit features of both the specific tourism destinations and the suppliers. Case 3 merely serves to illustrate the long-term advantages (and disadvantages) of tourism and travel operators in integrated promotional campaigns, and the responsibilities of their destination countries in developing both their similarities and unique differences in response to identified tourist markets. As crisis management theorists explain it, the "multi-linear, exponential and erratic patterns" (Rosenthal and Kouzmin, 1993, p. 5) of tourism provide significant challenges for governments, tourism industries, individual travel agencies, and tourism/hospitality operators. Although the framework provides few answers to these dilemmas, its primary purpose is to raise awareness of the multifaceted potential (and actual) vulnerability of the fragmented and segmented tourism industry throughout the Southeast Asian region, and by inference to alert astute tourism managers to some of the likely problems they face, and thence to suggest both short- and longer-term solutions to their dilemmas. As Rosenthal and Kouzmin (1993) put it, no other industry is so directly faced with the "sheer un-ness of crisis . . . un-scheduled, un-expected, un-planned, un-pleasant, sometimes un-imaginable and nearly un-manageable" (p. 5).

REFERENCES

Asian Business Review (1998). *Asian Business Review,* January 15, pp. 14-15.

The Australian (1997a). Devalued currencies cut prices for tourists. *The Australian,* August 23, p. 9.

The Australian (1997b). Economic worries deepen as pollution costs fall over tourism. *The Australian,* October 7, p. 29.

Australian Financial Review (1993). Tourism jitters. *Australian Financial Review,* January 6, p. 9.

Australian Financial Review (1997a). The burning issue. *Australian Financial Review,* October 6, p. 14.

Australian Financial Review (1997b). Asia aftershocks: More to come. *Australian Financial Review,* October 24, p. 92.

Australian Financial Review (1997c). Asian crisis threatens tourism jobs. *Australian Financial Review,* October 29, p. 36.

Australian Financial Review (1997d). Domestic tourism fears rush offshore. *Australian Financial Review,* October 30, p. 40.

Australian Financial Review (1997e). Asia shock hits tourism. *Australian Financial Review,* December 12, p. 42.

Business Review Weekly (1988). Vulnerable to a squeeze. *Business Review Weekly,* November 4, p. 6.

Courier Mail (1997). State fears tourism industry collapse. *Courier Mail,* October 29, p. 4.

Go, F. and Jenkins, C. (1997). *Tourism and Economic Development in Asia and Australia.* London: Cassell.

Griffin, T. and Darcy, S. (1997). *Australia—Consequences of the Newly Adopted Pro-Asian Orientation.* London: Cassell.

Hall, C. (1994). *Tourism in the Pacific Rim: Development, Impacts and Markets.* Melbourne: Melbourne.

Herald Sun (1996a). Pauline hits our pockets. *Herald Sun,* October 18, p. 21.

Herald Sun (1996b). Tourism fear over Hanson. *Herald Sun,* October 19, p. 9.

Heskett, J., Sasser, W., and Hart, C. (1990). *Service Breakthroughs: Changing the Rules of the Game.* New York: The Free Press.

Rosenthal, U. and Kouzmin, A. (1993). Globalizing an agenda for contingencies and crisis management: An editorial statement. *Journal of Contingencies and Crisis Management* 1(1): 1-12.

Rosenthal, U., t'Hart, P., and Kouzmin, A. (1991). The bureau-politics of crisis management. *Public Administration* 69(2): 212-233.

Seow, G., Tucker, K., and Sundberg, M. (1984). *Australian Trade in Tourist Services.* ASEAN.

Sydney Morning Herald (1997a). Concerns as hotels see 50 percent drop in Thai visitors. *Sydney Morning Herald,* October 23, p. 10.

Sydney Morning Herald (1997b). Tourism growth stymied by crisis in Asian markets. *Sydney Morning Herald,* November 7, p. 4.

Tisdell, C. (1995). Asian development and environmental dilemmas. *Contemporary Economic Policy* 13(1): 38-49.

Tourism Authority of Thailand (TAT) (1998). Visit Thailand, please. *Far Eastern Economic Review* 15: 51.

Travel Week (1997). Economic realism presents tourism opportunities. *Travel Week,* August 27, p. 4.

Usher, J. (1997). Flight or fright? *Time,* June 16, pp. 56-58.

West Australian (1997a). Crisis shock waves hit W.A. *West Australian,* October 25, p. 5.

West Australian (1997b). Asian problem to hit tourism sector. *West Australian,* October 31, p. 4.

Zeithaml, V., Parasuraman, A., and Berry, L. (1990). *Delivering Quality Service: Balancing Customer Perceptions and Expectations.* New York: The Free Press.

Chapter 5

Impacts of Tourism
on a Local Community:
A Case Study of Chiang Mai

Taksina Nimmonratana

INTRODUCTION

The tourism industry has a great deal of appeal for many countries, including Thailand. The reason is because of anticipated economic benefits such as income and employment. With these benefits, tourism is considered to be the country's top major foreign exchange earner and has contributed to the development of infrastructure. Jenkins (1997) stated that tourism is a service industry and relatively labor intensive, which is very important in the developing world where employment needs are substantial. It is also noted that major consumers of international tourism are from the developed countries which have hard currencies. Hard currencies are very beneficial to the developing countries as they help balance a trade deficit and contribute to overall development objectives. At the same time tourism can contribute a positive improvement to the infrastructure, which will benefit residents. For example, the new airport in Sukothai, built for Bangkok Airways, caters to tourists visiting the old city, and at the same time it has improved commercial links and communication for the residents.

However, the negative impacts of tourism are also observed. These impacts include social, environmental, and cultural changes such as drug trading, crimes, and changes in traditional arts and culture, high-rise buildings, and pollution. Social impacts involve immediate changes in the social structure of the destination and the destination's economy. But the community needs more time to absorb the the cultural changes (Murphy, 1985).

Tourism in Thailand was first recognized by the establishment of the Tourist Organization of Thailand (TOT) in 1959 and was upgraded and renamed the Tourism Authority of Thailand (TAT) in 1976 (Elliot, 1987). In 1977, tourism was for the first time incorporated into the National Economic and Social Development Plan, NESDP (Li and Zhang, 1997). However, the country became well known and acknowledged worldwide beginning in 1962 when U.S. soldiers first took "recreation and rest" leave in Thailand during the Vietnam War. Tourism, for the first time, played a leading role in the Thai economy in 1982 when it generated a revenue of 23,879 million baht, surpassing Thailand's traditional foreign exchange earner, rice (see Figure 5.1). Since 1982 tourism has been recognized as the country's top foreign currency generator.

Thailand is now competing with the magnificence of Angkor Wat, the grandeur of Borobodur, the forests of Malaysia, and the culture of Indonesia (Muqbil, 1995). Intensive competition among the tourist destinations within the region is one of the problems that

FIGURE 5.1. Tourism and Other Major Exports of Thailand 1981-1985 (Million baht)

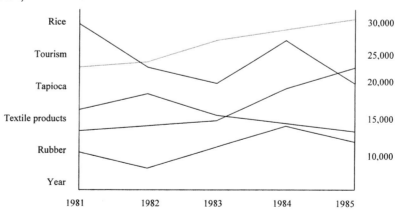

Source: The Tourism Authority of Thailand, 1986.

Asian tourism is facing (Qu and Zhang, 1997). In the new millennium, the TAT realizes consideration of global tourism trends is needed. Environment is the main issue the tourist industry should be aware of. The TAT also realizes that cultural virtues alone are not going to be enough of a unique selling proposition.

Chiang Mai, the second largest city after Bangkok and for decades the most popular destination in the north for both foreign and Thai travelers was chosen to be a study area of the impacts of tourism on local people.

CHIANG MAI: ITS LOCATION AND LANNA CULTURE

Chiang Mai province is situated 750 kilometers north of Bangkok (see Figure 5.2). Its north border is adjacent to Shan State in Myanmar. Its elevation is an average of 1,027 feet above sea level.

FIGURE 5.2. Map of Thailand

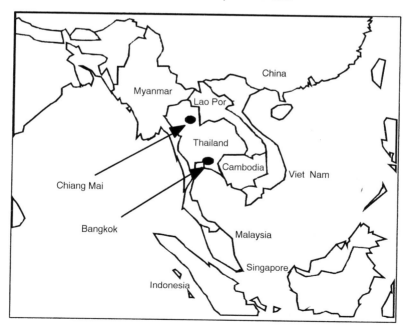

The average temperature is 21° Celsius, with humidity around 46 to 86 percent. There are three main seasons: the rainy season is from July to October; winter lasts from November to February; and the hot season extends from March to June.

The whole province has a total area of 20,170 square kilometers. It is mostly mountainous and forested and a smaller portion is plain plateaus for agriculture and residential areas (Khamhirund, 1994). The province consists of nineteen amphurs (districts) and three branch districts. Amphur Muang Chiang Mai (inner city) is the seat of provincial offices including the governor's office. The boundary of Chiang Mai is determined by the local administration, which has an area similar to Amphur Muang Chiang Mai.

The district of Chiang Mai or Amphur Muang Chiang Mai had a population of 354,129 people in 1992-1993. Ninety-seven percent of the people are Buddhist, 1.5 percent are Christian, and 1 percent are Muslim.

Chiang Mai is a rich city in historical terms. It has been established for about 700 years and has been considered the center of the Lanna Kingdom since the nineteenth century. The tourist activities in the city include touring the temple, sightseeing, trekking, and home product shopping. To realize the significance of Chiang Mai—how it is related to, but in many respects, distinct from, the rest of Thailand—a brief discussion about the evolution of the nation is required. During the early evolution of the Thai nation there were three kingdoms, Sukothai and Lanna, both founded in the thirteenth century, and Ayuddhaya, established in the fourteenth century. Sukothai and Ayuddhaya were both kingdoms of Thailand in those days. Sukothai was vulnerable and was absorbed by the more powerful Ayuddhaya in the fifteenth century, while Lanna, separated by its physical barriers, was not integrated into the Thai nation until later. A distinction between Lanna and the rest of Thailand persisted until the early twentieth century. Legend tells that the construction of Chiang Mai City was initiated by King Mengrai in 1296 after he seized states nearby in the northern region, such as Chiang Rai, Lumphun, and Phayao. The word "Lanna" meant the kingdom of a million rice fields, and Chiang Mai was used as Lanna's power base (Hoskin, 1989). The following paragraphs provide a brief introduction to traditional Lanna culture in the area of cuisine, dress, housing, and some traditional ceremonies.

Cuisine

A good introduction to northern cuisine is the Khan-toke dinner. Khan means "bowl" and "toke" means a small, low, round table made of wood. In traditional style, one sits on the floor around a table with a variety of dishes. A typical northern dish is always eaten with fingers instead of with a fork and a spoon as in central Thailand.

Dress

The Lanna dress style is unique among the northerners. Males usually wear "moh hom"—a collarless short-sleeved shirt with strings instead of buttons in the front and two pockets at the lower front part of the shirt. It is always a dark blue color made of native cotton. The trousers cover three-fourths of the leg length and are made from the same material. The trousers are very loose and are held to the body by a piece of cloth called "pa kao ma." This cloth is about the size of a beach towel; it is made of cotton and used for all purposes such as swimming trunks, a headband, face cloth, etc. Females usually wear sarongs made of cotton in horizontal stripes of color, usually in pale blue and white, or pale pink and yellow, or gray and pink. The lower part of the sarong is dominated by a stripe normally five times wider than the other stripes; the color of this stripe depends on the preference of the weaver. The blouse is normally white or off-white with buttons down the front. It may have short or long tapering sleeves. Women's hair is always pulled together in a bun at the crown of the head and decorated with orchids or some sort of silver ornament. This typical dress was adopted as the uniform for many hotels throughout Chiang Mai to give them a touch of Lanna Kingdom. Some geometrical patterns with assorted colors of thread may be seen as decorative patches on blouses.

Housing

Lanna houses are always made totally made of wood. Teak wood is preferable because of its durability and high tolerance to the weather conditions. Houses are supported by teak poles and the space underneath the house is always left open and used as a reception area or a weaving quarter, as well as a children's day care unit while their mothers are weaving nearby. The upper part of the house consists of a terrace, which leads to a common room and the bedrooms. The kitchen is actually in a separate building at the end of the terrace. Around the house in the upper floor are windows for good ventilation, and no air conditioning is needed. Near a wooden stairway which leads to the upper part of the house is an earthen jar containing water. It is customary to take one's shoes off and wash the feet with water before entering the house. The typical Lanna architecture is distinct from designs used in other parts of the country. The roof tiles are made from a typical terracotta of the north. "Galae" is a V-shaped design attached to the roof beams at both the front and the rear of the house. It consists of two pieces of wood crossing like a buffalo horn. The ends of both tips in the upper part of the horn are carved in a style called clouding scrolls or a wave or a flame pattern, depending on the intention of the wood carvers who try to put details in the carving art. Instead of "Galae," a carved triangular piece of wood, flowers, a peacock, or a rabbit may be placed in the front part of the gable as a typical decoration of the Lanna house.

Traditional Ceremonies

Lanna traditional ceremonies are deeply rooted in Buddhism. The ceremonies are always set up in the precinct of the temples and some are carried out along the main roads to let the people join in before the ceremonies end up in the temple again. The major ceremonies, which are popular and fun, are the Songkran festival (water throwing in the peak summer of April), and Loy Kratong festival, or a celebration of the full moon of the twelfth month. "Kratong" is a floating object made of a banana stem in a round shape normally about six inches in diameter, decorated with folded banana leaves and flowers. Candles and incense sticks are attached to the top of a kratong. People will make a wish and, at the same time, thank the river for providing water for them to use all year round. After a short prayer, the kratong is lighted and carefully tossed on the river.

TOURISM SITUATION IN CHIANG MAI

The advantageous location of Chiang Mai also provides a connection to nearby provinces, i.e., Chiang Rai and southern China. In fact, the terminal of the northern route of the railway system is in Chiang Mai, and it also has an international airport and a network of roads to nearby areas.

According to the statistics from 1995, 2,670,357 tourists visited Chiang Mai. This was a 12.39 percent increase over 1994, and the revenue accruing from this industry was 16,040 million baht (see Table 5.1).

TABLE 5.1. Number of Tourists Visiting Chiang Mai and Revenue 1992-1995

	No. of Foreign Tourists	No. of Thai Tourists	Revenue (million baht)
1992	789,453	1,083,844	13,752
1993	820,526	1,380,595	17,380
1994	886,000	1,489,974	16,400
1995	915,828	1,754,529	16,040

Source: Chiang Mai University, 1995.

Statistics from 1995 showed that people from Bangkok were the dominant Thais traveling to Chiang Mai, accounting for approximately 44.04 percent compared to visitors from other provinces. For the foreign market, tourists from Germany were the top rank, followed by France and Belgium, which produced a total percentage of 59.60. However, the TAT Chiang Mai branch predicts that the potential tourists will reach 4 million people with a contribution of 34,182 million baht by the end of 2001 (Chiang Mai University, 1995).

ANTICIPATED ADVANTAGES

Economic Effect

The study of Photiwaswarin (1993) indicated that during 1992 foreign tourists visiting Chiang Mai spent 3,375.94 million baht mostly on souvenirs and other products, followed by accommodation, entertainment, food and beverages, and transportation and sightseeing. These expenditures generated employment in Chiang Mai for 2,033 people. This number was then distributed in various business sectors related both directly or indirectly to tourism in Chiang Mai. The agricultural sector claimed to create the most employment, 56.655 percent, from foreign tourists, followed by nonmetal production sector at 19.282 percent, and the hotel and restaurant sector at 7.673 percent (see Table 5.2).

TABLE 5.2. Percentage of Employment Created by Tourism in Chiang Mai in 1992

	Foreign Tourists	Thai Tourists
Tourist Expenditure (Million baht)	3,375.94	7,209.35
Expenditure sectors (Million baht)		
Accommodation	826.44	1,634.36
Food and Beverages	518.20	1,157.11
Souvenirs	990.50	1,691.31
Entertainment	771.40	2,369.71
Transportation and Sightseeing	269.40	225.66
Others	0.00	131.19
No. of people employed	2,033	4,643
Sectors of employment (%)		
Agriculture	56.655	70.752
Nonmetal production	19.282	—
Service	—	9.692
Hotel and Restaurant	7.673	6.871

Source: Photiwaswarin, 1993.

In terms of Thai tourists visiting Chiang Mai, statistics for 1992 showed a total expenditure of 7,209.35 million baht, which was distributed mostly in entertainment, souvenirs, accommodation, food and beverages, and transportation and sightseeing. However, 4,643 were people employed both directly and indirectly in tourism.

Here again, the agricultural sector showed the highest percentage of employment (70.752), followed by the service sector (9.692), and the hotel and restaurant sector (6.871) (see Table 5.2).

The same study also stated that every 1,260,870.60 baht of foreign tourist expenditure in Chiang Mai generated one employed person, or that every 205 international tourists were able to generate one job. For Thai tourists, a spending level of 1,178,994.10 baht, or every 312 Thai tourists, could possibly generate one job.

Cultural Effect

When considering the cultural impact of tourism in Chiang Mai, it is observed that tourists have become patrons of particular cultural rituals and ceremonies or, as it is called, the Lanna tradition. These activities have become more widespread and schoolchildren are taught Lanna dance and music as well as the traditional Lanna style of dressing in elementary school. Sometimes Lanna dancers perform their folk dance in front of royal guests, demonstrating pride in their identity as local Chiang Mai. Smith (1978) indicated that the same feeling occurred in many young people in destinations where ethnic tourism prevails and has led many of them to celebrate their own traditions with continued vitality.

Some might argue that changes in manufacturing technique or in the material used to produce the art objects can shift or distort the old traditional style to the way tourists prefer (Chambers, 1991). The most ardent debate so far has been over the use of hill-tribe embroidery patterns decorating the Western style of women's jackets, which are sold at a relatively high price, just because they are partly handmade with a unique style from each tribe. This has been popular among Thais, especially when Her Majesty the Queen has shared her interest in promoting the hill tribe's needlework at the mobile work stations in the villages of the hill-tribe people around the suburb of Chiang Mai. Income accrued to Her Majesty the Queen's project is partly shifted back to the hill-tribe village to help them upgrade their living standard as well as create jobs with a guaranteed revenue. This project is widely known under the name SUPPORT. It is patronized by the queen and dedicated to providing a livelihood for village artisans specializing in jewelry, Thai silk, handicrafts, and paintings (Economic and Social Commission for Asia and the Pacific, 1994).

OBSERVED DISADVANTAGES

Economic Impact

It is widely accepted that when tourists come to Chiang Mai the circulation of money flourishes. However, the local people have noticed that the affluent foreigners and Bangkokians automatically push the food price in the market higher during the tourist season. The study of Sermsri (1986) showed the difference in average monthly income of people in tourist related and non-tourist related business in and outside the inner city of Chiang Mai.

The statistics showed a 50 percent difference in income accruing from tourism inside and outside the inner city of Chiang Mai. It confirms that local people in the inner city have to cope more with the increase of food prices and living costs than the people living outside (see Table 5.3).

Environmental Effects

Moonmuang Soi 1 is an alley situated in the heart of Chiang Mai city, where foreign tourists walk around collecting their laundry or

TABLE 5.3. Average Monthly Income in Families with Business Related to Tourism: Inside and Outside the City of Chiang Mai (Unit: Baht)

	Tourist Areas		Control Area
	In city	**Outside city**	
1. Total average income	7,801.64 (183)	5,154.93 (375)	3,537.93 (58)
2. Average income from tourism	7,959.38 (32)	2,841.67 (96)	800.00 (1)
3. Percentage of 2:1	102.0	55.1	22.6

Remark: ( ) Indicates number of people interviewed.

Source: Sermsri, 1986.

spend their time sipping a cold beer. This alley is also where tourists can find authentic Italian cuisine with homemade Italian bread from an Italian man who married a Chiang Mai girl. This alley used to be a quiet corner with a lot of lower-middle-class houses of local Chiang Mai. But after the tourism boom, many of them have been converted to cheap guesthouses or related businesses such as restaurants and laundries.

The major clients here are mostly limited-budget foreigners and young Japanese travelers. This alley produces a contrasting atmosphere: the first part is popular with lower-middle-income Thais, who gather at the typical northern food stalls; the middle part onward is a scene of houses converted to guesthouses or small hotels with a Western look of restaurants underneath. Since most of the clients here are foreigners, signs and advertisements are written in English and Japanese. During the day this area is quiet because some of the tourists go sightseeing or trekking, but the alley comes alive at dusk. For Thais, this alley gives a feeling of being somewhere else, not in Thailand at all.

Cultural Effects

In locations where contacts between hosts and guests are more continuous or permanent, changes of norms, values, and standards of hosts may occur, and these may be passed on to later generations; this is called genotypic behavior (Mathieson and Wall, 1982). The most visible example that supports this statement is the increased tendency of the hill tribes of northern Thailand to abandon their traditional forms of dress. Many of them learn that it can be traded to the tourists in exchange for cash, while some of them think that wearing a T-shirt is a sign of modernity (Dearden, 1991).

The village of Ban Thawai is another example of the growing integration of the village into regional, national, and international levels, which later causes a transformation of the village character. Cohen's (1996) study at Ban Thawai, which is located about 15 kilometers west of the urban center of Chiang Mai and is known as "carving village," revealed that the village consists of about 200 households, approximately 150 of which are engaged in craft production.

However, the villagers started to produce carved objects only a little more than twenty years ago. In the late 1960s, some Ban

Thawai villagers were employed by an antique shop in Chiang Mai doing restoration of Buddha images. After they acquired the necessary skills, the villagers moved back to the village and began to produce Buddha images and other religious statues. The skills were transmitted to other villagers, and later on the village became well known for the carving of such items. In the early 1970s the Thai authorities prohibited the export of Buddha images, compelling the producers to look for other lines of production. Now products at Ban Thawai range from Buddha images to Disney film characters.

METHODOLOGY

The survey research design selected for this study examined the perceptions of the large population living in the inner city of Chiang Mai regarding the impact of tourism. It used a survey questionnaire with a random sample taken from households in the area of Amphur Muang District (inner city), Chiang Mai Province.

A sample of 500 individuals was selected from residents of the inner city of Chiang Mai. The interview questionnaire was divided into two parts. The first part, which included eight questions, covered personal information on respondents, with mostly closed-ended questions. The second part of the questionnaire asked for opinions and perceptions of the respondents in eight major areas. Each had a different number of opinion categories to be explored (see Table 5.4).

Hypotheses are tested on the collected data as follows:

- The change in arts and culture can be noticed mostly by the older people
- Category of respondents by sex is not significant in explaining perceptions of local people
- Education is not an obvious indicator in testing the perceptions of local people
- Length of residency influenced positive or negative perceptions
- People engaged in tourist-related business have more positive opinions on the employment created by tourism
- Environmental problems are viewed negatively by local people
- Social problems are viewed negatively mostly by young people

TABLE 5.4. Computation of Indexes

Categorical Opinion Scores	No. of items	Range of Scores
1. Arts and culture	8	0 - 32
2. City environment	7	0 - 28
3. Modernization of city buildings	4	0 - 16
4. Infrastructure development	6	0 - 24
5. Employment in touring and sightseeing	3	0 - 12
6. Employment in accommodation sector and entertainment complex	6	0 - 24
7. Employment in souvenir shops	3	0 - 12
8. Social aspects within the inner city of Chiang Mai	3	0 - 12

Computation of Indexes

Seventy variables were obtained altogether from the questionnaire. They are finally grouped into eight independent variables that are related to personal characteristics of respondents (age and age group, sex, educational level, occupation, duration of stay in the city of Chiang Mai, immigration background, and knowing people in the tourism business (see Table 5.5), and forty-eight dependent variables (forty items of opinion and eight opinion scores). Eight opinion scores are further calculated according to the categorical aspects: (1) arts and culture; (2) environment; (3) modernization of buildings; (4) availability of the infrastructure; (5) employment in travel business; (6) employment in accommodation and entertainment business; (7) employment in souvenir shops; and (8) social aspects.

CONCLUSIONS WITH RELEVANCE TO THE HYPOTHESES

Based on the findings from the study, the first research hypothesis, stating that "the change in arts and culture can be noticed mostly

TABLE 5.5. Personal Characteristics of Samples

Characteristics	%
Sex of samples	
Male	44.8
Female	55.2
Age group of samples	
Less than 20 years old	6.2
20-39 years	60.4
40-59 years	29.8
60 years and over	3.6
Age distribution	
Mean	34.538
Standard deviation	11.995
n	500
Educational Level	
No education	1.8
Compulsory level	24.6
Secondary and high school levels	49.0
Bachelor and higher	24.6
Occupation	
Tourist related	.6
Private business	37.6
Government and skilled occupation	12.0
Farm and factory workers	36.7
Presently unemployed	13.1
Immigration background	
Native of Chiang Mai City	41.4
Immigrated from elsewhere	58.6
Duration of stay in Chiang Mai City	
Less than 20 years	46.6
20-39 years	35.4
40-59 years	16.6
60 years and over	1.4
Respondent and relatives involved in tourist business	
No one involved in tourist business	94.6
Respondent involved in tourist business	1.6
Relatives involved in tourist business	3.8

Note: Total sample = 500 people

by the older people," is accepted. The age of respondents affected the perception of change in arts and culture; older respondents were more aware of the decline of arts and culture. Accepted are the second and third hypotheses indicating that sex and education categories of the residents were not significant factors in testing perceptions. The educational variable in this study was ambiguous and showed no obvious relationship to the perceptions of the residents. Sex of the respondents also played no significant role in their perceptions of tourism's impact.

The fourth hypothesis, stating that length of domicile was an important factor in residents' perceptions, is accepted. Indeed, length of stay is the variable affecting the perception of tourism impact. The longer residents stay in the study area, the stronger attitudes they have.

The fifth hypothesis, indicating that residents with tourist businesses had more positive perceptions of employment created by tourism is accepted. Actually, residents expressed high positive perceptions of employment created by tourism, but respondents with tourist businesses tended to be more positive.

The sixth hypothesis, stating that environmental problems were viewed negatively by the majority of the respondents, is also accepted. The overall study showed that respondents viewed the environmental situation as being worse than before.

The last hypothesis, indicating that "social problems are viewed negatively mostly by young people" is not accepted. It was found that respondents between the ages of twenty and thirty-nine years tended to show strong negative attitude toward social problems, especially in the area of drug abuse.

POLICY ISSUES ARISING FROM THE STUDY

The study of local perception of tourism in the inner city of Chiang Mai can be summarized in five main issues as follows: First it is recognized that residents are the central focus of tourism planning. A community approach in tourism is therefore regarded as being equated with a region of local government.

As stated by Jenkins (1991), tourism is not only linked with sectors in the economy, but also has consequences of a social, cultural, and environmental nature. A number of organizations at different levels may play a major role in the development of tourism. The central government, the NTO, the local government, and most of all the community have to work together in formulating a tourism policy. Butler (1996) noted that tourism represents different things to different parties. Tourists expect to have enjoyment and pleasure; the government of the host country expects to have hard currency to reduce foreign debt; the local people need tourism to provide income and employment; and the community expects tourism to help preserve its natural and cultural heritage, and alleviate social and cultural problems resulting from tourist activities.

To serve the needs of every party as mentioned earlier, a community-based approach to tourism development should consider issues such as the local economy, the quality of development both culturally and environmentally, and most of all, the needs and potentials of the community and its people's needs. Tourism development can be positive to the community if its needs and interests are given priority over the goals of the industry (Brohman, 1996). The study of the North Pennines in the United Kingdom by Prentice (1993) also revealed that a community's homogeneity of view of tourism should be arrived at by shared decision making among residents.

However, in developing countries the idea of community involvement in tourism is very different than in Western countries, because decision making of many of these communities may be based on a traditional elite rather than on a community (Jenkins, 1996). For example, the redevelopment and revitalization of the ethnic enclaves of Chinatown, Little India, and Kampong Glam under the Tourism Product Development Plan of 1986 in Singapore were perceived by the local people as not identifying with the environment. People were dismayed to see the differentiation between the vernacular/local landscape and the elitist/government-supported landscape (Teo, 1994). In the case of Chiang Mai, the city was granted an Overseas Economic Cooperation Fund (OECF) loan from Japan between 1992 and 1995 for the improvement of footpaths around the inner city. Hexagonal concrete blocks replaced a cement footpath and white balloon-shaped lamp shades were hung on two-meter posts along the pavement by the inner city walls. The aim of the loan was to conserve and preserve the environment of the city, but the lamp shades seemed to be the target for slingshot users and rock throwers during the nighttime, turning the beautiful surroundings into an uncivilized area overnight. The people of Chiang Mai also widely discussed the unsuitable material used for the pavement as well as the height of the lampposts, which were tempting the street children to destroy them. The city improvement plan was drawn up solely by municipal officers without asking any opinion from the people.

Hall (1996) also expressed the same idea as the main difficulty in implementing a community approach to tourism planning; that is, decisions or the direction of decisions have already been prescribed by government. Thus, communities rarely have the opportunity to say no.

Second, residents' attitudes about tourism development in a community can vary significantly. Several studies indicate that people who have an economic gain from tourism perceive more positive impact from it. Along with the satisfaction of benefits, perceived costs are also associated with tourism. However, residents' positive attitudes are a function of tourism development. The type and scale of tourism a community wishes to have is a very important issue, which tourism planners and managers should take into consideration. The economic, social, and environmental perceptions should be aimed to meet the requirements of the residents.

As stated by Mill and Morrison (1985) the reasons for tourism planning are to protect the interest of both tourists and the host community. For a host country, planning should maintain the uniqueness of the local heritage; to avoid the undesirable, such as pollution and traffic problems, and to create a clear and positive image of the area. In the view of Jafari (1987), in the interest of the host country, tourists should absorb and pay for the impacts they leave behind.

It should be noted that overdevelopment can put pressure on the residents. Taylor (1995) referred to the residents as the "players within the community," and if they are pressurized by an increased number of visitors, it could result in widening community differences. It will lead to "annoyance" or "tolerance" when residents have uncertainty about the tourist industry and policymakers and show a degree of ambivalence toward tourism (Page, 1995). This stage of visitor-resident relationship is rather similar to the findings of this study, and it is the predictor for the Chiang Mai provincial authorities to take precautions before any development of tourism may lead the relationship between tourist and host to be categorized as "antagonism."

Third, in most developing countries including Thailand, the promotion of tourism to bring more tourists to the country is always the main aim of the government. Lately, it should be noted, the policies of both the government and the TAT emphasize cultural and environmental conservation and preservation. The concerned organizations should realize that it is no longer only the direct economic gains of tourism to be considered as a main criterion, but also the social, cultural, and environmental aspects. As noted by the United Nations Environment Program (1983, p. 53):

> There is almost universal agreement on the need to emphasize that, to the traditional criteria for economic efficiency—profitability of investments made—must now be added consideration of social and cultural effects.

Fourth, although the findings from fieldwork reveal many negative perceptions of local people toward the decline in Lanna arts and culture, the positive opinion is the increase of awareness and preservation of Lanna customs among school children.

The final main issue to be emphasized here is that young people are the group of local residents who will stay longest in the community. They are the essential component to encourage community-based tourism to grow at the pace and directions they wish it to. Local arts and culture are a significant tool to increase their awareness of being Lanna people via the school programs under cooperation from both public and private sectors. The Local Identity Enhancement model (see Figure 5.3) is introduced as the key way to strengthen Lanna arts and culture by focusing on the young people in the community. If the local identity is well preserved through understanding and cooperation between the concerned organizations, the direction and level of tourism development will be easier for the developers to follow; and this will ensure strong, positive attitudes of local people toward tourism.

Figure 5.3. Local Identity Enhancement

Source: Nimmonratana, 1997.

Cultural conservation was also viewed as a very negative aspect in the study. The awareness of Lanna culture can be built up among the local people, especially the young generations, through education. Here, local schools and universities as well as religious organizations can provide courses to train people for arts and culture or to organize special cultural events and festivals by emphasizing the history and preservation of Lanna arts. These can be on a competitive basis. Municipality, provincial government, and the Tourism Authority of Thailand (Chiang Mai branch) should act as the initiators. The private sector can offer support by sponsoring prizes and awards for the competitors. De Kadt (1979) expressed that the communities of developing countries, as in Bali and Bermuda, have little authority to deal with development; such powers were centralized, and local people have a limited chance to influence political decision making. The only way that local people can participate is through a process of education and increasing self-awareness. However, education is a strong recommendation, and it is a tool to enhance the awareness of people at every level in the community. The educational plan requires a low budget compared to other infrastructural investments and the assessment of each course is easier to evaluate; i.e., students know how to perform Lanna dance.

To maintain or to enhance the spiritual arts and culture of tourist-receiving destinations, Inskeep (1991) suggested that three parties

are involved, namely, community organizations, relevant government agencies, and religious organizations in that area. Education
about the local society and cultural traditions should be taught. It is
a continuous program in which modification is needed to cope with
change. Inskeep discussed Balinese culture as an example of the
involvement of the regional government to organize an annual cultural festival; dance, music, and crafts are judged on a competitive
basis. This was developed to maintain high quality and to prolong
or rejuvenate the arts and crafts of the country. As Ritchie (1993)
suggested, major events and programs in the community are the
venue that residents find most consistent with their values and
aspirations.

Figure 5.3 shows a possible interrelationship between organizations that could use an educational program to increase awareness
of the arts and culture of Chiang Mai. This program could be operated as part of the school program during term time. The educational
module can be initiated in primary school, but theory and practice
should be adjusted to suit students' age and ability; otherwise the
program will discourage them and lead to negative feelings.

Stressing economic gains from tourism may still be relevant to
the government of developing countries, but the following statement may give a second thought for a policymaker:

> International acceptance is just as necessary for a community
> as the self-respect that comes with the determination to protect
> its environment, preserve and develop its resources and hand
> down intact its culture and civilization to future generation.
> (IUOTO, 1992)

REFERENCES

Brohman, J. (1996). New direction in tourism for third world development. *An-
    nals of Tourism Research* 23(1): 48-70.
Butler, R.W. (1996). The role of tourism in cultural transformation in developing
    countries. In Nuryanti, W. (Ed.), *Tourism and Culture: Global Civilization in
    Change?* pp. 91-101.Yogyakarta: Gadjah Mada University Press.
Chambers, E. (1991). *Social and Culture Aspects of Tourism in Thailand: A
    Curriculum and a Study Guide.* Bangkok: Kasetsart University.
Chiang Mai University (1995). *The Statistical Report on Tourism in Chiang Mai*
    Chiang Mai: Chiang Mai University, Department of Statistics.

Cohen, E. (1996). "From Buddha Images to Mickey Mouse Figurines: The Transformation of Ban Thawai Carvings." Paper presented at Thai Studies, Chiang Mai University, Chiang Mai, Thailand, (October 6-14).

Dearden, P. (1991). Tourism and sustainable development in northern Thailand. *Geographical Review* 81(4): 400-413.

de Kadt, E. (1979). Social planning for tourism in the developing countries. *Annals of Tourism Research* 1: 36-48.

Economic and Social Commission for Asia and the Pacific. (1994). Review of tourism development in the ESCAP region. *ESCAP Tourism Review* 15, New York: United Nations.

Elliot, J. (1987). Government management of tourism—A Thai case study. *Tourism Management* 8(3): 223-232.

Hall, C.M. (1996). *Tourism and Politics: Policy, Power and Place.* England: John Wiley and Sons.

Hoskin, J. (1989). *Chiang Mai: The Tranquil Valley.* Bangkok: Artasia Press.

Inskeep, E. (1991). *Tourism Planning: An Integrated and Sustainable Development Approach.* New York: Van Nostrand Reinhold.

IUOTO (1992). *Charter for Development and Protection of Tourist Resources and Influence of Cultural Traditions on the Formation of Distinctive Supply.* Geneva: VIDOT Center International.

Jafari, J. (1987). Tourism models: The sociocultural aspects. *Tourism Management* 8(2): 151-159.

Jenkins, C.L. (1991). Tourism development strategies. In Lickorish, L.J., et al. (Eds.), *Developing Tourism Destinations: Policies and Perspectives,* pp. 61-78. Essex: Longman.

Jenkins, C.L. (1996). Incorporating cultural assets in tourism developing planning. In Nuryanti, W. (Ed.), *Tourism and Culture: Global Civilization in Change?* pp. 248-269. Yogyakarta: Gadjah Mada University Press.

Jenkins, C.L. (1997). Impacts of the development of international tourism in the Asian region. In Go, F.M. and Jenkins, C.L. (Eds.), *Tourism and Economic Development in Asia and Australia,* pp. 49-64. London: Cassel.

Khamhirund, J. (1994). *Planning, Management and Conservation: A Case of the Inner City Centre of Chiang Mai.* Bangkok: Mahidol and Silpakorn University.

Li, L. and Zhang, W. (1997). Thailand: The dynamic growth of Thai tourism. In Go, F.M. and Jenkins, C.L. (Eds.), *Tourism and Economic Development in Asia and Australia* pp. 286-303. London: Cassell.

Mathieson, A. and Wall, G. (1982). *Tourism: Economic, Physical and Social Impacts.* Essex: Longman.

Mill, R.C. and Morrison, A.M. (1985). *The Tourism System: An Introductory Text.* New Jersey: Prentice-Hall.

Muqbil, I. (1995). A time to travel new roads. *Economic Review Year-End 1995: The Bangkok Post,* pp. 41-43. Bangkok: Bangkok Post.

Murphy, P. (1985). *Tourism: A Community Approach.* London: Methuen.

Nimmonratana, T. (1997). "Local perception toward tourism in Thailand: A case study of Chiang Mai." PhD dissertation. Glasgow: University of Strathclyde.

Page, S. (1995). *Urban Tourism.* London: Routledge.

Photiwaswarin, S. (1993). "Economic effects of tourism industry in Chiang Mai vis-à-vis the whole kingdom." Master's of Economics Thesis. Chiang Mai: Chiang Mai University.

Prentice, R. (1993). Community-driven tourism planning and residents' preferences. *Tourism Management* 14(3): 218-227.

Qu, H. and Zhang, H.Q. (1997). The projection of international tourist arrivals in East Asia and the Pacific. In Go, F.M. and Jenkins, C.L. (Eds.), *Tourism and Economic Development in Asia and Australia,* pp. 35-47. London: Cassell.

Ritchie, B. (1993). Crafting a destination vision: Putting the concept of resident-responsive tourism into practice. *Tourism Management* 14(5): 379-389.

Sermsri, S. (1986). *Social and Cultural Impact of Tourism: A Case Study of Chiang Mai.* Bangkok: Mahidol University.

Smith, V.L. (1978). *Hosts and Guests: The Anthropology of Tourism.* Oxford: Blackwell.

Taylor, G. (1995). The community approach: Does it really work? *Tourism Management* 16(7): 487-489.

Teo, P. (1994). Assessing socio-cultural impacts: The case of Singapore. *Tourism Management* 15(2): 126-136.

United Nations Environment Program (1983). Workshop on environmental aspects of tourism.

Chapter 6

An Analysis of Tourism Flows Between Australia and ASEAN Countries: An Australian Perspective

Bruce R. Prideaux
Stephen F. Witt

INTRODUCTION

Prior to the financial crisis that swept through a number of Asian nations in 1997, the ASEAN countries were emerging as the star performers in Australia's strategy of diversifying its Asian tourism source markets away from Japan. In the period from 1985 to 1997, the share of total inbound tourism to Australia from the nations comprising the original ASEAN block (Indonesia, Thailand, Singapore, Philippines, Malaysia, and Brunei) increased from 8 percent to 15 percent. Conversely, outbound tourism to the ASEAN countries from Australia declined in overall percentage terms from 4.4 percent in 1989 to 3.7 percent in 1995 (although the actual number of tourist visits increased slightly). The Tourism Forecasting Council (TFC), established by the Australian Federal Government in 1995 to provide an independent and specialized source of tourism forecasting, predicted that the share of Australia's inbound market sourced from the larger ASEAN countries of Thailand, Indonesia, Singapore, and Malaysia would increase from 14 percent of total inbound visitors (601,000) in 1996 to 19 percent (1,474,000) by 2004 (Tourism Forecasting Council, 1997a). Projections were built on the premise of a continuation of the high rates of growth achieved over the previous ten years. Apart from the impact of the controversy caused by the 1996-1997 so-called "race debate" in Australia inspired by the anti-Asian comments of independent member of Federal Parliament Pauline Hanson, the TFC forecasts appeared to be on target during the first six months of 1997. The TFC projections also appeared to be in line with the general expectations of researchers (Qu and Zhang, 1997; World Tourism Organization [WTO], 1994; World Travel and Tourism Council, 1996) that the long-term pattern of tourism growth, based on continuing economic growth, would continue into the foreseeable future. The Asian financial crisis that commenced in mid-1997 set in motion a series of events that has disrupted the tourism industry in many ASEAN countries. Taken together with the forest fire-generated smoke haze that affected Indonesia, Singapore, and Malaysia in late 1997, as well as concerns about weaknesses in the Chinese economy, the continuing poor performance of the Japanese economy, and political unrest in Indonesia, the Asian financial crisis is likely to continue to have a significant impact on tourism flows between Australia and the ASEAN countries, as well as among the ASEAN nations themselves, at least in the short term.

This study examines the development of tourism flows between Australia and the ASEAN countries over recent years, and comments on the possible impacts of the financial crisis on the future course of tourism flows. The chapter is structured in two parts. The first part takes a historical perspective, examining the development of tourism between Australia and the ASEAN countries up to 1997. It concludes with a review of the forecasts made for tourism growth prior to the emergence of the currency crisis. The second part of the chapter takes a more speculative stance, examining a range of issues that is likely to affect the future development of tourism demand between Australia and the newly expanded ASEAN group (including Vietnam). Trends and events commented upon in this part of the chapter reflect the course of the financial crisis up to August 1998. While the discussion centers on the causes and continuing impacts of the financial crisis, other factors, such as the residual effects of the "race debate" in Australia, uncertainty over the course of the Japanese economy, political unrest in Indonesia, the possible long-term impacts of the Indonesian forest fires, and changes in the north Asian economies, are also considered. Discussion in the first section is based on official statistics released by national governments and compiled by the World Tourism Organization and published research reports and growth estimates made by the TFC. In subsequent sections a much broader group of sources is used, including news reports and official press releases, reflecting the recent nature of the phenomena being analyzed.

DEVELOPMENT OF TOURISM
BETWEEN AUSTRALIA AND ASEAN UNTIL 1997

Prior to the emergence of Japan as a significant source of inbound tourism, Australia's primary marketing activities were focused on New Zealand, the United Kingdom, and the United States of America. The emergence of the Japanese economy as a major force in world trade in the 1970s forced a reevaluation of Australia's tourism marketing strategies and a recognition that Asia was destined to grow in significance as a new source of tourists. Following in the wake of Japan came other newly industrialized Asian nations, including Korea, Singapore, and Hong Kong. Australians, already familiar with Asia as a result of increased Australian outbound tourism to Asia commencing in the 1970s, were generally comfortable with large numbers of Asian tourists visiting the country. This represented a considerable change in public attitudes for a country that just a decade earlier had divested itself of the "White Australia" immigration policy that had restricted Asian immigration for over a century.

As the federal government recognized to a greater extent the value of tourism as an export sector, it increased the funds available to the Australian Tourism Commission (ATC) for promotion. At the same time, led by Queensland's state tourism office, the Queensland Tourist and Travel Corporation (QTTC), state governments recognized the significance of Asia and increased their promotional efforts, including the establishment of state tourism offices in a number of Asian countries. Results of the attention given to Asian markets soon became apparent as Asian arrivals increased rapidly. Growth patterns for the 1985-1997 period are illustrated in Table 6.1.

Inbound tourism to ASEAN countries has also increased over the 1987-1995 period as illustrated in Table 6.2. As far as Australian

TABLE 6.1. International Visitor Arrivals in Australia 1985-1997 by Source Country (000s)

	North America	Europe	New Zealand	Japan	ASEAN*	Other Asia	Rest of World	Total	Annual Increase (%)
1985	237	300	245	108	81	163	89	1223	
1986	292	347	337	146	110	204	103	1539	25.8
1987	362	412	427	216	137	255	113	1922	24.9
1988	389	531	534	354	162	308	135	2413	25.5
1989	315	531	449	350	155	321	114	2235	− 7.4
1990	304	549	418	480	177	171	116	2215	0
1991	325	531	481	529	197	192	116	2371	7.0
1992	312	577	448	630	257	244	131	2599	9.6
1993	332	637	499	671	354	350	154	2997	15.1
1994	344	721	480	721	456	471	169	3362	12.2
1995	363	752	538	783	526	592	172	3726	10.8
1996	378	799	672	813	601	710	192	4165	11.8
1997	394	874	686	814	612	738	200	4318	3.7
Total % Increase 1985-1997	166	291	280	754	756	453	225	353	

*Arrivals from Thailand, Singapore, Malaysia, and Indonesia.

Source: Tourism Forecasting Council, 1998.

arrivals in the ASEAN countries are concerned, in recent years Australians have widened the scope of their travel horizons to include Malaysia, Thailand, Singapore, and Indonesia, as these destinations have enhanced the quality of the tourism experience they have been able to offer.

Prior to the Asian financial crisis, forecasters were unanimously predicting strong economic and tourism growth in the region until well into the first decade of the twenty-first century. For example, the World Tourism Organization (1996, cited in Singh, 1998) forecast that tourism in the Asia-Pacific region would grow at an annual rate of 7.6 percent to number 229 million international arrivals in 2010, making the region the world's second largest tourism region after Europe. In a 1996 report, the World Travel and Tourism Council projected that by 2006 Southeast Asia would generate 3.9 percent of world gross output of travel and tourism services, up from 2.5 percent in 1996. These forecasts are similar to those that have been made by a number of researchers, including Qu and Zhang (1997). A comparison of the prefinancial crisis forecasts for inbound tourism to Australia (Tourism Forecasting Council, 1995) with the

TABLE 6.2. Arrivals at Borders of ASEAN Countries of Tourists from Abroad 1987-1997 (000s)

	1987	1988	1989	1990	1991	1992	1993	1994	1995	1996	1997
Philippines											
Total	795	1,043	1,190	1,025	951	1,152	1,372	1,574	1,760	2,049	2,222
SE Asia	47	60	64	48	49	51	60	70	76	87	132
Australia	44	45	51	47	44	55	68	84	76	87	94
Cambodia											
Total	N/A	N/A	N/A	N/A	N/A	N/A	118	177	220	261	219
SE Asia							26	32	38	59	55
Australia							8	7	7	8	7
Malaysia											
Total	3,359	3,624	4,846	7,446	5,847	6,016	6,503	7,197	7,469	7,138	7,200
SE Asia	2,615	2,779	3,800	5,495	4,155	4,516	4,883	5,431	5,542	5,206	N/A
Australia	90	99	76	149	122	121	122	128	136	150	N/A
Singapore											
Total	3,679	4,186	4,830	5,323	5,415	5,990	6,426	6,899	7,137	7,292	6,542
SE Asia	1,074	1,158	1,257	1,443	1,554	1,700	1,822	2,024	2,055	2,098	N/A
Australia	333	36	450	457	367	345	333	322	325	334	N/A
Indonesia											
Total	1,060	1,301	1,626	2,178	2,570	3,064	3,403	4,006	4,324	5,034	5,036
SE Asia	354	476	614	848	1,082	1,225	1,340	1,519	1,705	1,799	2,124
Australia	133	147	163	179	219	235	288	305	320	380	418
Thailand											
Total	3,483	4,231	4,810	5,299	5,087	5,136	5,761	6,167	6,952	7,192	7,660
SE Asia	1,098	1,227	1,120	1,224	1,278	1,210	1,259	1,357	1,719	1,613	1,714
Australia	111	138	199	227	203	208	197	193	201	224	266
Vietnam											
Total	N/A	N/A	N/A	N/A	N/A	440	600	1,018	1,351	1,607	1,716
SE Asia						10	14	24	23	20	N/A
Australia						N/A	N/A	N/A	N/A	N/A	N/A
Myanmar											
Total	N/A	N/A	N/A	N/A	23	27	48	80	110	165	185
SE Asia					5	6	4	12	12	17	N/A
Australia					1	1	1	2	3	3	3
Brunei											
Total	411	523	457	393	344	412	489	622	498	837	850
SE Asia	379	492	426	363	314	379	454	581	N/A	N/A	N/A
Australia	2	2	2	2	4	3	3	3	7	8	7

Source: World Tourism Organization, 1993, 1997, 1998b.

revised postfinancial crisis forecasts (Tourism Forecasting Council, 1998) is illustrated in Tables 6.3 and 6.4, and indicates that less than 35 percent of the tourist visits from Asia expected previously are now forecast to materialize during the period 1998-1999.

Estimates of future patterns of tourism growth assume great importance when they form the basis for investment decisions, ranging from the purchase of a minibus by a tour operator to a multi-billion dollar investment in new airports by national governments.

TABLE 6.3. Original TFC Projections of Visitor Arrivals in Australia 1998-2003 (000s)

	Indonesia	Malaysia	Singapore	Thailand	Total Asia	Total World
1998	292	196	309	171	2895	5197
1999	347	223	336	203	3254	5699
2000	394	249	363	235	3623	6299
2001	440	274	387	264	3981	6761
2002	484	306	407	288	4282	7219
2003	512	332	424	309	4502	7581

Source: Tourism Forecasting Council, 1995.

TABLE 6.4. Revised TFC Projections of Visitor Arrivals in Australia 1998-1999 (000s)

	Indonesia	Malaysia	Singapore	Thailand	Total Asia	Total World
1998	48	86	241	34	1822	4114
1999	48	91	252	42	1951	4356

Source: Tourism Forecasting Council, 1998.

However, tourism forecasting is a notoriously difficult task, as illustrated by the large differences between the 1995 and 1998 TFC forecasts, and as noted previously by Crouch (1994) and Witt (1992). Many of the events that have occurred in Asia during the course of 1997 and 1998 were simply not forecastable; nevertheless, forecasting is a vital element in tourism planning.

Factors responsible for the growth of outbound tourism from Asian countries include: increases in personal disposable income based on strong national economic growth; development of national travel agency networks; easing of travel restrictions; air transport liberalization; increased political stability; professionalization of the region's travel industry; and increased marketing by government-supported NTOs and the private sector (Singh, 1998). Australia's ability to capture a share of this emerging market centered on a number of factors including: increased promotion by the ATC and state tourism offices such as the QTTC; a development boom in the construction of resort properties, hotels, and golf courses in the 1980s; increased Japanese investment in hotel and resort development; prodevelopment agendas of state governments; redevelopment or construction of new international airports at Cairns, Brisbane, Sydney, and Melbourne; a rapid expansion of tourism and hospitality training courses at the postsecondary level; the staging of major events of international interest such as Expo 88, the Bi-Centenary of the first white settlement, and sporting events including the Indy car race and golfing classics; the willingness of financial institutions to lend funds for tourism-related investment; development of new transport and communications infrastructure; and a relatively lenient immigration system, which encouraged Asians to migrate to Australia as well as enabling Asians to work in Australia on short-term permits.

Prior to the financial crisis, the only factors that appeared to have any potential to reduce tourism demand between ASEAN and Australia were the smoke haze originating from uncontrolled forest fires in Sumatra and Borneo, and the Hanson factor. Although the anti-Asian views of Pauline Hanson were widely reported in a number of Asian countries, the impact was short lived and ultimately overtaken by the financial crisis. Similarly, the smoke haze appeared to have limited impact on overall tourism numbers and ceased to be a factor after their extinguishment by the annual monsoons.

Whereas tourism markets seemed to be locked into a continuous cycle of development, spurred on by new resort and hotel development and general confidence in the future, developments in the region's financial markets began to cast a shadow over the optimism of the tourism industry in early 1997. The ensuing financial crisis forced forecasters to revise their projections in line with the fall in tourist arrivals from mid-1997. Following the recent economic upheavals, the precrisis projections by the TFC (Tourism Forecasting Council, 1995, 1997a) and the projections developed by the World Tourism Organization (1994) are clearly overoptimistic.

CAUSES OF THE FINANCIAL CRISIS

The financial crisis commenced with the devaluation of the Thai baht in July 1997 when Thailand renounced the pegging of its currency to the U.S. dollar (Chong, 1997). Unable to restore confidence in the baht, the Thai government requested assistance from the International Monetary Fund (IMF). IMF intervention in Thailand unleashed a massive attack on currencies throughout the region, which eventually resulted in IMF intervention in Korea and

Indonesia. Malaysia escaped IMF intervention through timely and prudent government action but did not escape a significant devaluation of the rinngit. The crisis resulted in large falls in currency values against the Australian dollar between May 1997 and March 1998 of 34 percent for the Thai baht, 22 percent for the Malaysian rinngit, 74 percent for the Indonesian rupiah, 20 percent for the Philippine peso, and 6 percent for the Singapore dollar. At first, the Australian dollar fared reasonably well, falling 16 percent against the U.S. dollar, but was later to suffer a twelve-year low as a consequence of the May political crisis in neighboring Indonesia.

The factors that caused the financial crisis fall into several categories and include: the continuing weakness of the Japanese economy; the fundamental belief in the inherent strength and even superiority of the so-called "Asian Model" as a way of business (Kersten, 1998); and a range of other factors which sparked the lack of confidence by the international money markets that led to the attack on the value of Asian currencies. Initially, the underlying cause of the crisis appeared to lie with the assumption by Asian leaders, both political and business, that the so-called Asian model, based on strong government intervention, protectionist policies to insulate sectors of the national economy from international competition, cronyism, lack of transparency in business reporting to stockholders, and government-sanctioned monopolies, all hallmarks of the corporatist state, would continue to underpin national development agendas into the postindustrial phase of economic development. By late June 1998, the continuing weakness of the Japanese economy emerged as the most likely contender for the long-term cause of the crisis. Japanese unwillingness or inability to reform its banking sector in the wake of the bursting of the "property bubble" in 1991 led to weak or zero growth in the ensuing six years (Landers and Biers, 1998). The failure of government stimulatory polices to reignite consumer spending during this period, allied with weak demand for imports, has removed the engine of growth factor that had earlier underpinned much of the growth in Asian economies.

The immediate causes of the financial crisis differ slightly between countries, but a number of common factors can be observed: the failure to decouple national currencies from the U.S. dollar when the U.S. dollar began to appreciate against the yen and European currencies in 1996-1997; weak financial sectors allied with a lack of independence of central banks; reliance on short-term foreign borrowing for infrastructure development by the private sector rather than direct foreign investment or long-term bond issues; and difficulty servicing overseas debt. These conditions contributed to imprudent lending practices where resources were misdirected into sectors that had failed to perform well (Downer, 1998a), resulting in the buildup of large numbers of poorly performing loans and high levels of corporate debt in the private sector. As a result, currency traders stepped up their speculative activity against the currencies in the first half of 1997, leading to massive currency devaluations. Initially, as the values of the currencies appreciated, the cost of exports rose while that of imports fell, leading to increased unemployment and worsening balance of payments conditions. Later on, as the currency values fell, the cost of servicing short-term debt increased markedly.

Both Thailand and Korea have implemented the IMF conditions imposed on them and in both countries the precrisis governments have lost office with an orderly succession of administrations. Indonesia has wavered in its implementation of reforms, and the continuing lack of confidence by the international money markets appeared to move from concern about the country's economic problems to a loss of confidence in the Suharto government. The concern centered on the Suharto government's apparent inability to separate the business interests of family and so-called cronies from the national interest. Some commentators (Kelly, 1998; Dalrymple, 1998) have noted that the conditions imposed on Indonesia have gone beyond the need to restore confidence in the rupiah, and appear to render the concept of national sovereignty obsolete by transforming the IMF into an agent of market-oriented liberalism. The dispute between the IMF and the Suharto government, allied with a high level of internal unrest, partly attributable to increased prices insisted on by the IMF, saw the Suharto government fall. The success of new President Habibie in restoring domestic and international confidence in the Indonesian economy, and its success in renegotiating a fourth IMF rescue package, will affect the stability of the entire region and determine the recovery of domestic and international tourism.

In the Western economies, the changes that are just starting to occur in Asian financial markets were initiated nearly twenty years previously, and had their roots in the deregulationist policies of President Ronald Reagan in the United States and Prime Minister Margaret Thatcher in the United Kingdom. Australia has also undergone the types of policy changes that have now been forced on the Asian economies by the IMF, commencing with the floating of the Australian dollar in 1983 and financial deregulation of the Australian banking sector in the 1980s.

Impact on ASEAN Nations

The currency turbulence in the ASEAN nations, followed by financial reforms imposed on Thailand, Indonesia, and Korea by the IMF, has had a number of effects on the domestic economies of the nations concerned, including a substantial reduction in GDP growth, increased unemployment, and a rise in inflation. These effects spilled over into political life, as occurred in Indonesia in early 1998 when riots and looting occurred in over forty towns in reaction to a reduction in food subsidies insisted on by the IMF and to dissatisfaction with the policies of the Suharto government. A further series of riots, widespread looting, and numerous deaths accompanied the resignation of President Suharto, forcing foreign governments to place military assets on a state of alert for possible evacuations.

As one of the first sectors to feel the effects of economic disruption, the tourism industry throughout the region has begun to report a fall in inbound and outbound tourism demand. Examples of the severity of the crisis are evident in the latest tourism statistics from the region. Inbound tourism to Singapore commenced falling for the first time in fourteen years in October 1997, and by January 1998 was down 17 percent on the same month in 1997 (Eaton, 1998). Malaysia experienced a 19 percent decline in 1997, and falls also occurred in Vietnam and Indonesia. Australia suffered significant falls in inbound tourism from ASEAN countries as well as Korea, commencing in the last few months of 1997. For example, inbound travel to Australia in December 1997, compared to December 1996, was down 25 percent from Thailand, 45 percent from Indonesia, 21 percent from Malaysia, and 6 percent from the Philippines (Australian Tourism Commission, 1998). In the light of the financial crisis, the International Air Transport Association has revised its passenger traffic growth forecasts for 1996-2001, as illustrated in Table 6.5. The World Tourism Organization (1998a) has also revised its three-year forecast for Asia, estimating that in the period 1997-2000, 11 to 12 million potential tourist arrivals will be lost.

In Asia, the impact of the currency upheavals may produce a mix of negative and positive results in the short term. Because travel to long-haul destinations such as Europe and the USA will become more expensive as a consequence of the currency devaluations, it is possible that there will be an increase in intra-ASEAN tourism flows if local prices do not rise as quickly. Furthermore, ASEAN countries should be able to benefit from the fall in their currency values by being able to market cheaper holidays to residents of countries not involved in the currency problems (particularly North America and Europe), as well as those affected to only a limited extent (such as Australia). This has already become apparent in Thailand, where tourism fell by only 0.03 percent in the period from January to November 1997 (Ainsworth, 1998a). In this case, although Asian and some European arrivals were down, arrivals from Australia increased by 9 percent and New Zealand by 6 percent. In Indonesia, Bali recorded a 50 percent increase in inbound tourism from Australia in 1997, based on heavy price discounting by tour operators and the increased purchasing power of the Australian dollar in Indonesia (Alford, 1998). Negative impacts arising from the financial crisis are likely to include reduced profits, job losses, declines in business travel, declines in tax revenues, and a rise in the failure rate of firms trading in the tourism sector. The uncertainty generated by the effects of the financial crisis has also affected the ability of NTOs and private sector operators to develop reliable tourism forecasts. Concerns over the future course of events in Indonesia, the possibility of a Vietnamese financial crisis (Huckshorn, 1998), and uncertainty about the future direction of Japanese economic policy create major difficulties for forecasters. The alternative approach of developing forecasts based on a series of scenarios of what might occur was recently employed by the Tourism

TABLE 6.5. IATA'S Annual Passenger Traffic (Inbound Plus Outbound) Growth Forecasts, 1996-2001 (Percent)

	Previous Forecast	**Revised Forecast**
China	14.0	11.7
Taiwan	11.2	7.0
Japan	5.8	4.1
Korea ROK	8.1	3.1
Malaysia	8.0	4.8
Singapore	7.2	5.1
Thailand	7.3	4.0

Source: PATA, 1998.

Forecasting Council (1997b) and may offer a viable short-term alternative.

In its initial response to the financial crisis, the Thai government substantially reduced government expenditure, including tourism promotion. However, by early 1998 the Thai government, recognizing the economic significance of tourism, instituted a number of policies to stimulate tourism. These included ordering government agencies and state enterprises to ease obstacles for the tourism industry, tightening controls on safety aspects of water sports and adding tour vehicles, instituting new controls on tour companies and tour guides, and adding measures to protect tourists from exploitation by the local tourism industry (Ainsworth, 1998b). Some sectors of the Thai hotel sector have attempted to capitalize on the devaluation of the baht by charging in U.S. dollars. The "dollar trap" greatly increases the return to operators in Thai baht, but reduces the overall benefit to the country that can be derived from reduced tourism costs. The Thailand Tourism Society has responded by urging hotel prices to be quoted in baht (Ainsworth, 1998b).

Impact on Australia

The effects of the currency crisis are already evident in Australia. As the exchange rate for a number of ASEAN currencies has fallen against the Australian dollar, travel from Australia to Asia has become cheaper while travel from Asia to Australia has become more expensive. The Tourism Forecasting Council (1997b) issued its first revision of forecast inbound Asian tourism demand (excluding Japan) in December 1997, predicting falls of up to 5 percent. These figures already appear conservative, based on the 12 percent fall in ASEAN tourists in December 1997 compared to December 1996 (Australian Bureau of Statistics, 1998). In general, the effects for Australia are likely to include increasing outbound tourism to ASEAN countries, a fall in inbound travel from ASEAN countries, job losses in major tourism destinations dependent on Asian tourism, an increase in bankruptcies of firms servicing the inbound tourism industry, a decline in tax revenue from tourism-related businesses, and an increase in the balance of trade deficit.

The impact of the financial crisis on tourism-related businesses is already evident in the airline industry (see Table 6.5) and sections of the accommodation industry. In January 1998, Quantas canceled a number of flights to Indonesia and Thailand, as well as suspending all flights to Korea, while Ansett Australia announced the cancellation of flights to Malaysia and Jakarta in May 1998. On the Gold Coast, a popular destination for many Asian visitors (both independent travelers and those on inclusive tours), hotel room rates commenced falling in late 1997 in response to a fall in international arrivals and an emerging oversupply condition. Room rates continued to fall in 1998 as Asian arrivals declined. Employment in the tourism industry had already started to contract by February 1998. Results of a survey conducted by the Australian Bureau of Statistics and published in *The Australian* (Kersten, 19C8) indicated that employment in accommodation, cafes, and restaurants fell from 412,000 in February 1997 to 395,000 in February 1998, a reduction of 17,000 jobs. In the same article, the Tourism Council of Australia is reported as stating that the council estimated that total job losses were likely to be on the order of 40,000, and revenue from overseas visitors had declined considerably. A further indication of the impact of the financial crisis was contained in the 1998-1999 Australian federal budget, which forecast that economic growth in Australia would decline from 4 percent per annum to 3 percent per annum as a consequence of the financial crisis (Dwyer, 1998). The domestic tourism industry may also suffer, as travel to destinations in

ASEAN countries becomes cheaper than travel to upmarket resort properties and destinations in Australia, although some Australian states have recently initiated marketing strategies to increase their domestic tourism market (Wright, 1998). Anti-Suharto riots in May 1998 had further significant short-term consequences.

It can be anticipated that Indonesian inbound tourism to Australia, which stood at 160,000 in 1997, will evaporate in the short term and only resume when political stability and growth resumes. Other inbound markets may also suffer if potential visitors fail to distinguish between the trouble in Indonesia and stability in nearby Australia.

For the Australian tourism industry, the response by the Australian government has been disappointing. During the initial stages of the crisis, the government appeared to be in a state of denial asserting that the financial crisis would have only minimal impact. For example, the federal minister for tourism voiced sympathy over the impact and suggested that tourism operators should take advantage of the increase in Australia's competitiveness as a consequence of the fall in the value of the Australian dollar by seeking to concentrate marketing activities in North America and Europe. No additional funding was made available for this suggested promotion. Australia will not be alone in targeting the North American and European markets, with Asian nations also seeking to attract visitors from this region. Moreover, North America is currently the target of intense competition from other destinations including the Caribbean, Africa, and Latin America (World Tourism Organization, 1998a).

Even after the impact of the crisis became evident, the response of the government was muted. In the federal budget announced on May 13, 1998, funding for the ATC was increased by AUD$12 million per year; however, these funds were to be collected from an increase in the airport departure tax that will raise estimated additional revenue of AUD$20 million per year (Dwyer, 1998). In view of the decline in government revenue that will occur as the number of inbound tourists falls, and the increased cost of unemployment benefits paid to retrenched tourism workers, the response is mystifying.

Long-Term Impacts

The long-term impacts of the Asian financial crisis on the tourism industry are much harder to estimate and will largely depend on the post-financial crisis rates of economic growth achieved in ASEAN and other Asian countries undergoing economic difficulties. Countries most affected by the crisis will need to adjust their economies through increased trade liberalization, including encouragement of foreign investment, improved prudential controls, and transparency of company balance sheets (Downer, 1998b). The future direction of the Japanese economy will have a major impact on regional economic activity. If the Japanese economy emerges from its current malaise, the effects will quickly flow throughout the region in the form of increased business activity and additional Japanese outbound tourism. Conversely, if the Japanese economy continues to stagnate, the restoration of economic prosperity in Asia will take longer. A Japanese economy in recession will drag surrounding economies, including Australia, into either minimal growth or possible recession. The ability of the U.S. economy to continue to fund large current account deficits, partly funded by high Japanese domestic savings, is also critical. If the U.S. can maintain its ability to soak up cheap Asian imports, a speedy Asian recovery is more likely.

A further factor of some importance is the direction and pace of reform in the Chinese economy, particularly the state-controlled banking sector, which is reported to have a significant amount of nonperforming loans (McGregor, 1998). Chinese President Jiang Zemin has stated that China will not devalue its currency to regain its competitive advantage over other Asian nations and will also reform the country's financial sector. However, falling exports and the cost of lost production and repairs to flood-damaged regions of the Yangtze River basin as a result of a series of floods in July and August 1998 may cause Chinese authorities to reconsider their policy of not devaluing the yuan. Changes to these policies or pressure from the international financial sector could reignite lack of confidence and cause further declines in Asian currencies. If a parallel is drawn with the outcome of the previous IMF intervention in Latin America in the 1980s and early 1990s and the more recent bailout of Mexico in 1994, it is apparent that the quicker the Asian nations adjust their economies through trade liberalization, greater prudential controls, and transparency in both the public and private sectors, the faster they will overcome their present difficulties and return to high growth rates. Ultimately, the long-run outcome should be positive and lay the foundation for a resumption of strong growth built on a revitalized banking sector (AFP, 1997).

In August 1998, the fall in the value of the Russian ruble also began to exert an influence on the world economy, as commodity-based economies such as Australia, New Zealand, Canada, South Africa, and Latin America experienced attacks on the values of their currencies by investors and traders. By the end of August 1998, the value of the Australian currency fell to its lowest level since the AUD$ was floated in December 1983. Continued uncertainty in financial markets will impact on recovery in ASEAN countries, as well as increasing the possibility of reduced economic growth in Australia. Such reduced growth would result in increased unemployment and, allied with a weaker Australian dollar, would reduce the opportunity for ASEAN countries to look to Australia as a source of additional tourists.

Domestic responses to the currency crisis will also have an impact on the region's tourism industry, particularly if political structures come under pressure and civil unrest emerges, as occurred in Indonesia in May 1998 when student-led protests escalated into widespread civil unrest, looting, and anti-Chinese riots. The Indonesian unrest generated a new round of uncertainty in world financial markets that resulted in a fall in the value of the rupiah and, driven by adverse market sentiment, also caused the Australian dollar to fall against the U.S. dollar. Images of riots, department stores burning in uncontrolled fires, police beatings of demonstrators, and announcements by government authorities in Australia, Japan, and the United States of plans to use military assets to evacuate their nationals added to the perception that the region encompassing Australia and ASEAN is not safe for tourists. Effects are likely to be short lived, however, as history shows that if public order and stability is restored quickly, the initial drop in inbound tourism will be followed in the longer term with a resumption of business as usual. In Asia, this postcrisis condition was observed after the infamous Tiananmen Square massacre in Beijing in 1989, the failed coup in Cambodia in 1997, and Corazon Aquino's 1986 people-power revolution in the Philippines.

A further factor of some concern in the near future is the ability of the Asian economies to generate the funds, and the will, to face up to the task of implementing strategies to combat the anticipated impact of the year 2000, or millennium bug (Y2K). Failure to achieve high levels of compliance in correcting computer software problems in key tourism-related sectors may lead to serious problems emerging in 2000. Airlines, reservation systems, financial services, and the myriad other services that support tourism may be affected, causing a serious lack of confidence in key inbound tourism markets. Such a scenario could be regarded as a ripple effect of the financial crisis.

CONCLUSION

For Australia and the ASEAN countries, efforts to boost tourism will require implementation of well-developed strategies that must target the short term as well as the long term, include consideration of the supply side and demand side, and be based on the assumption that other nations will also be attempting to increase their market shares (Prideaux, 1998). For example, Australia could seek to build up its North American and European markets, while the ASEAN countries could concentrate on shorter intra-ASEAN holiday travel. Tourism authorities in both ASEAN and Australia should not be tempted to abandon all promotional activity in the worst-affected countries, because in the medium to long term these countries should emerge economically stronger. Failure to service these markets in the short term by low-key promotion, such as advertising in the trade press and popular media, as well as maintenance of close personal ties with members of the travel trade, may result in the postcrisis outbound tourism industry seeking other markets. The need for governments to maintain funding for NTOs, at least at current levels, is crucial for the region's tourism industry. Reducing funding will achieve short-term savings but can easily be translated into the loss of valuable markets and associated loss of government revenue in the long term.

Industry must also play a significant role in the postcrisis recovery. Pressure on governments to increase financial and legislative assistance will be required, as will expressions of confidence in the form of new investment. Business will need to learn from previous mistakes and strive to increase the quality of service offered to tourists. The immediate postcrisis period will also afford businesses the opportunity to refocus on the needs of the customer and adjust their products and services to cater to emerging consumer demands such as sustainable tourism, more emphasis on individual needs, and the development of MICE (Meetings, Incentives, Conventions, and Exhibitions) tourism.

The Asian financial crisis also highlights the need for additional funding for tourism research, particularly in the areas of tourism forecasting and the development of greater understanding of the impact of economic forces on the tourism industry. Specific issues that could form part of a research agenda include contingency planning, scenario development, the relationship between tourism demand and economic forces, and changing patterns of demand for holiday travel.

REFERENCES

AFP (1997). Asian crisis a blessing in disguise, says IMF. *The Australian,* November 4: 29.

Ainsworth, N. (1998a). Thailand skates on the edge while tourists cash in. *Travelweek,* March 4: 22.

Ainsworth, N. (1998b). Thailand looks to tourists to kickstart economy. *Travelweek,* May 13: 33.

Alford, P. (1998). It's a tough job but someone has to save Bali. *The Weekend Australian,* March 21-22: 1.

Australian Bureau of Statistics (1998). *Overseas Arrivals and Departures Catalogue No 3401.1.* Canberra: Australian Bureau of Statistics.

Australian Tourism Commission (1998). *Tourism Pulse No. 69,* Sydney: ATC.

Chong, F. (1997). Curing Asia's currency contagion. *The Australian,* October 16: 40.

Crouch, G.I. (1994). The study of international tourism demand: A survey of practice. *Journal of Travel Research,* 32(4): 41-56.

Dalrymple, R. (1998). World is underestimating Indonesian crisis. *The Australian,* March 11: 13.

Downer, A. (1998a). Globalisation or globaphobia: Does Australia have a choice? *Foreign Affairs and Trade Record,* 2(1), Australian Department of Foreign Affairs and Trade: 5-7.

Downer, A. (1998b). East Asian transformations: Challenges for Australia. *Foreign Affairs and Trade Record,* 2(1), Australian Department of Foreign Affairs and Trade: 15-18.

Dwyer, M. (1998). Asia impact: 1pc cut in GDP. *The Australian Financial Review,* May 13: A7.

Eaton, D. (1998). Cheaper Asia no lure. *The Sunday Mail,* March 8: 124.

Huckshorn, K. (1998). Vietnam on brink of fiscal meltdown. *The Courier Mail,* March 19: 20.

Kelly, P. (1998). IMF tightens the screws on Suharto. *The Australian,* March 11: 13.

Kersten, R. (1998). Capital gains from culture. *Inside Asia, The Australian,* April 20: 42.

Landers, P. and Biers, D. (1998). This will hurt. In D. Beirs (Ed.), *Crash of 97: How the Financial Crisis is Reshaping Asia.* Hong Kong: The Far Eastern Economic Review.

McGregor, R. (1998). Zhu Keen on Keynesian plan. *Inside Asia, The Australian,* April 20: 10.

PATA (1998). IATA revises forecasts for Pacific Asia air traffic growth. *Hotel Online Press Release* (Online), <http://www.hotel-online.com/Neo/Trends>.

Prideaux, B. (1998). Australia's response to growth in Korean outbound tourism since 1989. In S.O. Lee and D.S. Park (Eds.), *Perspectives on Korea* (pp. 33-51). Sydney: Wild Peony.

Qu, H. and Zhang, H.Q. (1997). The projection of international tourism arrivals in East Asia and the Pacific. In F. Go and C.L. Jenkins (Eds.), *Tourism and Economic Development in Asia and Australia.* London: Cassell.

Singh, A. (1998). Asia Pacific tourism industry: Current trends and future outlook. *Asia Pacific Journal of Tourism* (Online), <http://www.hotel-online.com/Neo/Trends/AsiaPacific Journal Asia>.

Tourism Forecasting Council (1995). *Forecast,* 1(2). Canberra: Office of National Tourism, Commonwealth Department of Industry, Science and Tourism.

Tourism Forecasting Council (1997a). *Forecast,* 3(2). Canberra: Office of National Tourism, Commonwealth Department of Industry, Science and Tourism.

Tourism Forecasting Council (1997b). *Short, Sharp Shock or Lower Growth Outlook?* Canberra: Office of National Tourism, Commonwealth Department of Industry, Science and Tourism.

Tourism Forecasting Council (1998). *Forecast,* 4(1). Canberra: Office of National Tourism, Commonwealth Department of Industry, Science and Tourism.

Witt, S.F. (1992). Tourism forecasting: How well do private and public sector organizations perform? *Tourism Management,* 13(1): 79-84.

World Tourism Organization (1993). *Yearbook of Tourism Statistics,* 2. Madrid: WTO.

World Tourism Organization (1994). *Global Tourism Forecasts to the Year 2000 and Beyond: East Asia and the Pacific,* 4. Madrid: WTO.

World Tourism Organization (1997). *Yearbook of Tourism Statistics,* 2. Madrid: WTO.

World Tourism Organization (1998a). *Report to the WTO Commission for East Asia and the Pacific.* Thirty-Second Meeting, Koyoto, February 18. Madrid: WTO.

World Tourism Organization (1998b). *Yearbook of Tourism Statistics,* 2. Madrid: WTO.

World Travel and Tourism Council (1996). *The 1996/7 WTTC Travel & Tourism Report.* London: World Travel and Tourism Council.

Wright, J. (1998). Sydney launches tourism offensive on Southern Queensland. *The Courier Mail,* March 9: 7.

Chapter 7

Coastal Tourism in Southeast Asia: Research from the Environmental Perspective

Poh Poh Wong

INTRODUCTION

To the average person, coastal tourism is associated with sun, sea, sand, and resort comfort. From a research point of view, coastal tourism represents the interaction of a human system (tourism) and an environmental system (coast). The interaction of these two systems involves a wide variety of human and environmental aspects (Wong, 1991). Most studies on coastal tourism emphasize the tourism system rather than the environmental system and the interaction between these two systems. Also, many studies tend to focus on resort land use and morphology and on the patterns and processes of coastal tourism (Pearce, 1995; Burton, 1995).

This chapter summarizes the results of the author's ongoing field research on coastal tourism in Southeast Asia from an environmental perspective initiated in the mid-1980s. The emphasis is on aspects that are of an applied nature. Various examples illustrate the progress and results of this line of investigation.

COASTAL TOURISM IN SOUTHEAST ASIA

Compared to Europe and North America, coastal resorts are relatively new in Southeast Asia. They are a postwar phenomenon and

Note: The bulk of the fieldwork in Southeast Asia was supported by three research grants from the National University of Singapore. Other data were collected during the course of commission work.

they developed very rapidly in the 1960s and 1970s. The better known international resorts include Bali, Pattaya, Phuket, and Penang. Others such as Ko Samui, Langkawi, Lombok, and Cebu are now beginning to attract international attention. Innumerable minor resorts are also utilized mainly by domestic tourists; for example, those in the Gulf of Lingayen cater to residents of Manila.

Studies on Southeast Asian coastal resorts focused initially on various economic, social, and cultural impacts of coastal tourism, in which Bali has attracted more attention than other resorts (Universitas Udayana and Francillon, 1975; Francillon, 1979; Noronha, 1979; Hussey, 1989; Picard, 1996). Spanning across the national scale, other studies deal with their evolution (Franz, 1985; Smith, 1991), planning and development issues (Smith, 1992a, 1992b), and their context within coastal zone management (Wong, 1998).

ENVIRONMENTAL PERSPECTIVE

One of the initial steps of field research on coastal tourism in Southeast Asia was to examine the extent of the environmental perspective in case studies and regional works. It quickly became obvious that the environmental aspects were often little considered or underestimated.

In the field, it was found that the coastal environment was not fully understood or appreciated by the developers of the resorts. For example, buildings were insufficiently set back from the beach, sea walls were constructed unnecessarily, thus encouraging beach erosion, and river mouth dynamics were underestimated. Also, the effects of the monsoons or seasonal winds were sometimes underestimated or ignored in coastal tourism development.

COASTAL GEOMORPHOLOGY

As the coast is a basic component of coastal tourism, it should be understood as fully as possible. Coastal tourism development may vary, depending on the intrinsic physical bases or coastal resources available. For example, resorts on small islands differ from resorts perched on rock coasts or located in a large sandy bay backed by an ample hinterland. Specific advantageous and disadvantageous physical attributes, such as abundant coral reefs, coastal dunes, sand spits, river mouth bars, and rocky headlands can influence substantially the choice of resort sites and the pattern and development of resorts.

Coastal geomorphology, the study of coastal processes and landforms, provides a basic understanding of the coastal environment as illustrated in two studies. In the first study, the resorts on the east coast of Peninsular Malaysia were evaluated in the field according to a number of criteria including the location and layout of the resort buildings and facilities, various aspects of the coastal environment, the types of vegetation, the influence of rivers, and the role of monsoons (Wong, 1990). This study identified and evaluated five major types of coasts and their suitability for beach resort sites: zetaform bay, nonzetaform bay, coastal or barrier spit, low linear coast, and estuary (see Figure 7.1).

Each coastal type has distinctive advantages and disadvantages for the location of the resorts. In the zetaform bay, the most sheltered area is in the curved sector and the exposure to waves increases southward along the straight sector. The possible resort sites are in the more sheltered northern curved sector, not too close to the headland and away from a stream outlet; along the straight sector but away from a stream outlet; and set back at the southern end of the straight sector where the exposure to waves is high. In the nonzetaform bay, the most suitable resort site is the central sector of the bay where minimal beach changes take place. The strong seasonal beach changes preclude sites near the headlands.

The barrier spit found along the Trengganu coast offers three possible sites for resorts: landward of the permanent channel (river), landward of the seasonal channel, and at the area where the spit merges with the mainland. Existing chalets on the coastal spit are subject to the impacts of the northeast monsoon. For the low linear coast, the preferred resort sites should be away from any coastal erosion and river mouths. Within an estuary the resort site should be raised above the high-water mark and away from the changes attendant on spit formation.

In the second study, a geomorphological survey was carried out on the north coast of Bintan Island for integrated resort develop-

FIGURE 7.1. Coastal Types and Beach Resort Sites, East Coast of Peninsular Malaysia

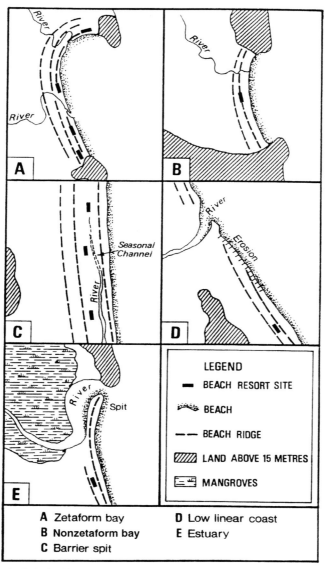

ment. This produced an inventory of the coast on 1:20,000 maps showing various coastal types (sandy shore, rocky shore, coral reefs, mangroves, disturbed shore, island) with supplementary information on stream outlets, coastal erosion, and beach profiles and grain size changes of twenty-four stations for three monsoon seasons. Based on the field survey, it was possible to evaluate various aspects of the coastal environment relevant to tourism development: the sandy beaches, rocky headlands, boulders, rivers, coral reefs, coastal vegetation, relict sand ridges, and setback lines.

The geomorphological survey of the north Bintan coast provides valuable information for coastal tourism in several areas:

- Suitable resort sites, for example, low-lying bays between the headlands, straight "permatang" or sand ridge beach, and picturesque pocket beaches along a highland coast, including some unique locations (a horseshoe-shaped bay fringed by a coral reef with a narrow channel approaching near to the beach)
- Sensitive areas to be avoided, for example, small islands, certain headlands, coastal sectors with fringing reefs or live corals, and mangrove areas
- Some idea of the seasonal beach changes and the setback lines to be taken
- Preliminary data for the environmental impact statement (EIS) required by the integrated resorts

Islands

Tropical islands with their insularity and unique combination of landforms and water and year-round sunshine are particularly attractive for resort development. Many well-known coastal resorts in Southeast Asia are island resorts.

The island size is one of the critical factors influencing the development of tourism. A study of small islands off the east coast of peninsular Malaysia showed that several environmental aspects were of particular importance to island tourism (Wong, 1993). These can be summarized in a schematic representation of small island tourism (see Figure 7.2).

The northeast monsoon has a strong influence on the island, restricting suitable sandy beaches and tourism development to the

FIGURE 7.2. Schematic Representation of Small Island Tourism

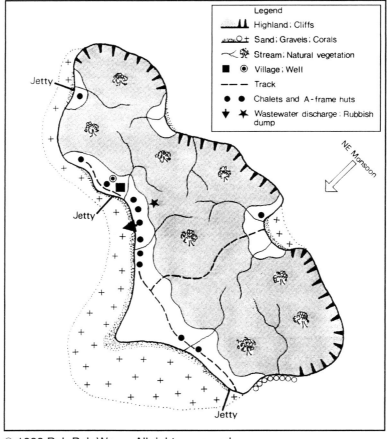

sheltered west coast. Some resorts are closed during the northeast monsoon. Accessibility to the islands was initially dependent on fishing boats visiting the islands. For the more developed and popular resort islands, a ferry service is available. Jetties are built across the coral reef flats on the sheltered west coast. Accessibility on the island is by footpaths and tracks, although some isolated tourist beaches are only accessible by boat. On most islands, the original forests have been replaced by a secondary vegetation cover. The island's resources are limited. The water is supplied by wells but they have become increasingly saline due to a lowering of the water table, and the islands rely on potable water brought in jerry cans by boats. All food supplies have to be imported except for limited amounts of coconut, fish, and poultry from the local fishing village. Tourism development is typically spontaneous and operates on a small scale based on chalets or A-frame huts. The negative impacts of such development are evident in the inadequate setback from the beach, the discharge of wastewater into the sea, and rubbish dumps hidden in a vegetated area out of sight from the tourists. From an environmental perspective, the important aspects of small-island tourism include accessibility, the limited resources of water, the problem of waste disposal, and the distinctive difference between the sheltered and the exposed coasts.

Bays

With many Southeast Asian coastal resorts preferring bay-type locations, bays between headlands represent an obvious choice to investigate the relationships between the coastal environment and tourism development. The west coast of Phuket Island provides a suitable study area as varying levels of tourism development are found in eight bays of different sizes. Patong, Karon, and Kata are the most developed touristically; Bang Thao is the largest bay and has an integrated resort; Kammala, Surin, and Nai Harn have a lower level of tourism development; Laem Sing virtually has no tourism development. This study is a further amplification of the interaction between the human and physical systems. The results of this interaction were summarized on a schematic map and the intensity of various changes (graded light, medium or strong change, no change, or not applicable) was compared for the eight bays (see Table 7.1) (Wong, 1995).

Although this study did not extend into the developmental pattern of tourism of each bay, several observations can be made on the following major changes: provision of access, removal of vegetation, removal of beach ridges, construction on the backshore, provision of coastal protection, and changes to streams and stream out-

TABLE 7.1. Tourism-Environment Interaction, West Coast Bays, Phuket

	LS	SR	NH	KM	BT	KT	KR	PT
Provision of accessibility	~	~	~	*	*	#	#	#
Removal of natural vegetation	~	*	~	*	*	#	#	#
Removal of beach ridges	n	~	#	~	*	*	*	n
Construction on backshore	~	~	n	*	*	*	*	#
Provision of coastal protection	n	~	~	~	*	*	*	*
Changes to streams	—	~	—	~	*	*	#	*
Others	—	—	—	*	—	—	*	—

— No change
~ Light change
* Medium change
# Strong change
n Not applicable

LS Laem Sing
SR Surin
NH Nai Harn
KM Kammala
BT Bang Thao
KT Kata
KR Karon
PT Patong

Source: Wong, 1993.

lets. The results of this study have implications for the planning and management of tourism in such bays: the question of access and the setback of the coastal road, minimum removal of the vegetation cover and beach ridges, attention to the stream mouths, avoidance of sea wall construction, and prohibition of the discharge of wastewater into the bay.

Rock Coasts

Although sandy beaches are still available in Southeast Asia as sites for resorts, rock coasts have also been utilized for tourism development. In particular, rocky headlands provide vantage viewpoints, although construction costs are higher. Mactan Island, opposite Cebu City, is composed of limestone. Its southeast coast provides an opportunity to examine resort development on a low rock coast with limited sand beaches.

Since the 1970s, resorts have been developed on Mactan's southeast coast, which also has two lagoons. Given the increasing demand for sandy beaches, the rock coast and the two lagoons have been physically transformed in various ways by the resorts. Three major changes to the rock coast for both the exposed sector and the lagoon can be identified, and they followed the general development of the resorts (see Figure 7.3) (Wong, 1998). The initial stage involved a minimum change to the rock coast and the beaches in which sea walls and rock bunds were used. The middle stage witnessed a variety of coastal structures to retain the beaches and beach nourishment. Groins are the main structures and together with breakwaters, a variety of resort layout is created. The final stage is the excavation of the rock coast and the lagoon and the creation of artificial beaches.

Mactan's experience shows the potential and extent to which a low rock coast can be used for resort development. Much depends on the deployment of appropriate coastal protection measures, beach nourishment, and the success of artificial beaches (grain size is critical). Tourism development on a rock coast remains essentially enclave in character, that is, the resorts are isolated from one another. This is in contrast to the more prevalent ribbon development of tourism along sandy beaches where the resorts developed adjacent to one another

FIGURE 7.3. Use of Low Rock Coast for Tourism, Mactan, Philippines

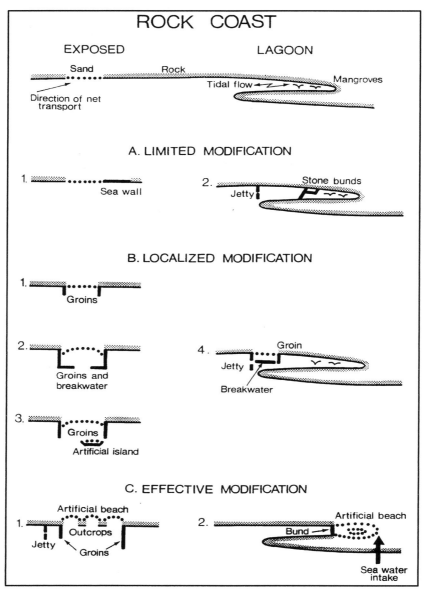

along the coast. There is also the need to maintain the coastal structures and artificial beaches on a transformed rock coast.

Coastal Erosion

On several tourist coasts of Southeast Asia, coastal erosion appears to be a major problem, and coastal protection is therefore necessary. On other tourist coasts, the evidence for coastal erosion is less evident, but sea walls have been built to protect the resorts. The obvious question is: how and to what extent are coastal erosion and coastal protection related to tourism development?

From an environmental perspective, it would be interesting to find out if tourism development is a significant anthropogenic factor in coastal erosion. From an evaluation of references covering coastal tourism, three main sets of factors appear to be significant in influencing the evolution of tourist coasts: the physical character of the coast, the nature and extent of the tourist development, and the shore protection works that are related to tourist development or as a response to a beach erosion problem.

Bali presents an ideal situation to examine these questions. The major tourist beaches at Kuta, Jimbaran, Sanur, Nusa Dua, Candi Dasa, and Lovina have different physical characteristics, experienced varying types of tourism development, and have a wide variety of coastal protection measures. Field mapping and observations were carried out on the physical nature of the coast, the nature and extent of tourism development, and shore protection measures. Each tourist coast was subdivided into sectors where necessary; an example is given for the Sanur coast (see Figure 7.4).

This study provides a simple classification and further identification of tourist coasts into sectors based on the field observation of three sets of factors. The identification of the sectors depends on one predominant factor or a combination of two or three factors. A tourist coast is likely to start as a single-sector coast based primarily on the physical factor. Multiple sectors subsequently result from the nature and extent of tourism development and the deployment of coastal structures. This implies that in the evolution of the tourist coast, the latter two factors become more important and have to be considered. The original physical factor is likely to remain constant or decrease in significance in the evolution of the tourist coast.

FIGURE 7.4. The Tourist Coast of Sanur, Bali

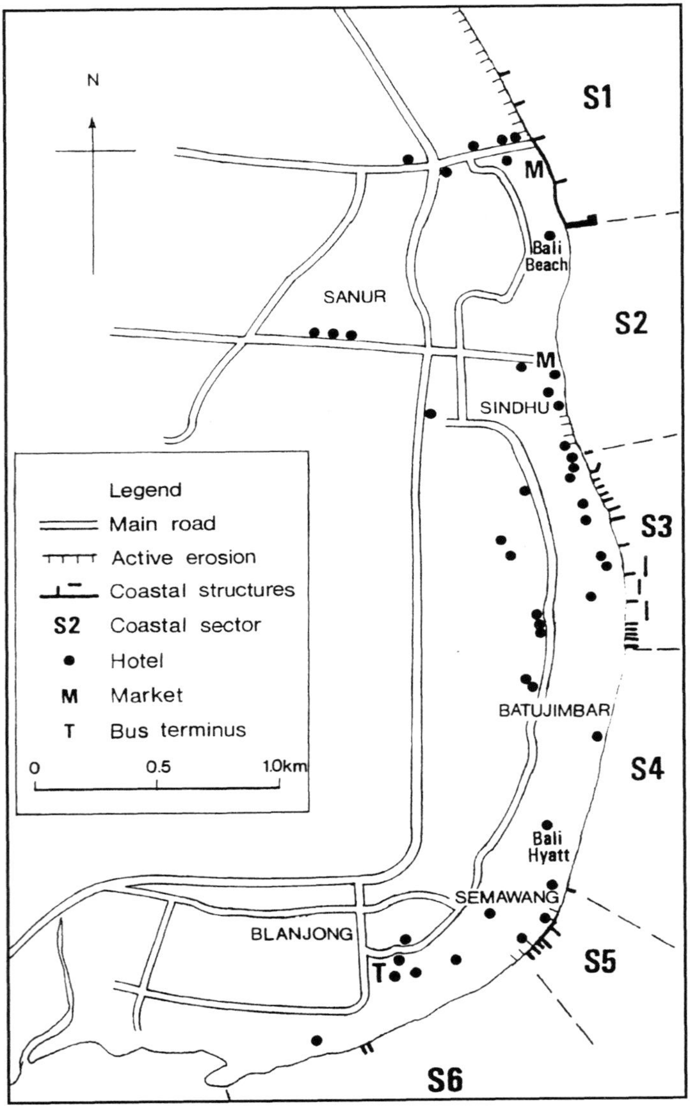

The field research shows that the coastal protection measures on Bali's tourist coasts are deployed in three possible situations:

- Measures to protect resort properties primarily from beach erosion due to natural and artificial causes. Seawalls and groins are the most common measures.
- Specific and successful measures to provide the coastal environment required by the tourists, for example, breakwaters to provide protected waters at Club Med, and groins to protect artificial beaches at Bali Hotel and Pertamina Cottages.
- "Last-resort" measures to salvage the coastal environment for coastal tourism, a case of "too late to save the situation." For example, at Candi Dasa, large T-groins are used to protect a coast that has lost its beaches due to the destruction of the fringing coral reef and the construction of sea walls.

With the rise of coastal tourism development, the tourist coast will become increasingly important in Southeast Asia. The tourist coast generally evolves from a physical base but is further transformed by the extent of tourist development and coastal protection measures. In its transformation, the problem of coastal erosion, if present, has to be assessed properly. From the environmental perspective, the tourist coast has to be further subdivided for a more detailed evaluation. The study from Bali adds to the understanding of this issue in the nature and evolution of the tourist coast.

FUTURE ENVIRONMENTAL RESEARCH

As more Southeast Asian countries implement environmental impact assessment for development projects, environmental research on coastal tourism will continue and become increasingly important. Future research is likely to be on the following areas:

1. *Setback lines.* Usually, a single setback line is legislated within the country, making it easy for administrative purposes and for implementation. But coastal environments are complex, thus necessitating sometimes a reduction or increase in the setback distance. A variable setback line is more realistic for coastal

tourism development, but this requires detailed field evaluation of the coastal environment. Malaysia is considering different set-back lines for the islands and also taking into consideration the sea level rise resulting from global climate change.

2. *Environmental assessment guidelines.* These have to be determined clearly and the standards enforced. Although most countries have some form of environmental impact assessment for development projects, few have specific EIAs for coastal tourism and related projects. In the future, coastal resorts in Southeast Asia may face further environmental guidelines imposed from outside the region, arising from a number of European initiatives related to consumer rights and the environment. For example, a scheme to implement guidelines for safe swimming beaches, similar to the European Blue Flag program, is possible. The bad publicity on the polluted water at Boracay has shown the urgency for such action.

3. *Sustainable coastal tourism development.* This is still a debatable topic and will require continued research inputs from the environmental perspective. The major issues center on the scale of tourism development, benefits to the local population, and the implementation of sustainable tourism. There is also a move away from the carrying capacity approach to management strategies to accommodate growth with minimal adverse impacts. Less faith seems to be placed in the notion that community involvement will contribute significantly to sustainability (Griffen and Boele, 1997). As yet there is no universal applicable model for coastal sustainable tourism development. The environmental perspective can help to identify "best practices" in relation to sustainable tourism development.

CONCLUSION

This chapter has indicated several areas of research on coastal tourism in Southeast Asia, taken from the environmental perspective. The work was partly a response to the lack of such information and also to balance or complement other approaches. Coastal geomorphology and field work are essential in this perspective, which will continue to contribute their value to coastal tourism development.

REFERENCES

Burton, R. (1995). *Travel Geography,* Second Edition. London: Pitman.

Francillon, G. (1979). *Bali: Tourism, Culture, Environment.* Universitas Udayana and UNESCO.

Franz, J.C. (1985). The seaside resorts of Southeast Asia (part one). *Tourism Recreation Research* 10(2): 15-23.

Griffen, T. and Boele, N. (1997). Alternative paths to sustainable tourism: Problems, prospects, panaceas and pipe-dreams. In F.M. Go and G.L. Jenkins (Eds.), *Tourism and Economic Development in Asia and Australasia* (pp. 321-337). London: Pinter.

Hussey, A. (1989). Tourism in a Balinese village. *Geographical Review* 79: 311-325.

Noronha, R. (1979). Paradise reviewed: Tourism in Bali. In E. de Kadt (Ed.), *Tourism—Passport to Development?* (pp. 177-204). Oxford: Oxford University Press.

Pearce, D. (1995). *Tourism Today: A Geographical Analysis,* Second Edition. Burnt Mill: Longman Scientific and Technical.

Picard, M. (1996). *Cultural Tourism and Touristic Culture.* Singapore: Archipelago Press.

Smith, R.A. (1991). Beach resorts: A model of development evolution. *Landscape and Urban Planning* 21: 189-210.

Smith, R.A. (1992a). Coastal urbanization: Tourism development in the Asia Pacific. *Built Environment* 18(1): 27-40.

Smith, R.A. (1992b). Review of integrated beach resort development in Southeast Asia. *Land Use Policy* 9: 209-217.

Universitas Udayana and Francillon, G. (1975). Tourism in Bali—its economic and social-cultural impact: Three points of view. *International Social Science Journal* 27: 721-752.

Wong, P.P. (1990). The geomorphological basis of beach resort sites—some Malaysian examples. *Ocean and Shoreline Management* 13: 127-147.

Wong, P.P. (1991). *Coastal Tourism in Southeast Asia.* ICLARM Education Series 13. Manila: International Center for Living Aquatic Living Resources Management.

Wong, P.P. (1993). Island tourism development in Peninsular Malaysia: Environmental perspective. In P.P. Wong (Ed.), *Tourism vs. Environment: The Case for Coastal Areas* (pp. 83-97). Dordrecht: Kluwer Academic Publishers.

Wong, P.P. (1995). Tourism-environment interactions in the western bays of Phuket Island. *Malaysian Journal of Tropical Geography* 26(1): 67-75.

Wong, P.P. (1998). Coastal tourism development in Southeast Asia: Relevance and lessons for coastal zone management. *Ocean and Coastal Management* 38: 89-109.

Wong, P.P. (1998). Adaptive use of a rock coast for tourism, Mactan Island, Philippines. *Tourism Geographies.*

Chapter 8

Preconditions for Successful Collaborative Tourism Marketing: The Critical Role of the Convener

Jutamas Jantarat
Lesley Williams

INTRODUCTION

In the past forty years, there has been a phenomenal growth in international tourism. This is despite the world economic instability of the 1980s (Harrison, 1992) and the recent financial crisis of the 1990s. Many international organizations, such as the United Nations and UNESCO, as well as individual economists, have, in fact, stressed the economic benefits to be gained from utilizing a country's natural and cultural heritage to provide a large source of foreign exchange earnings (Picard, 1996). Tourism can play an important role in this process, as well as indirectly assisting national infrastructure development, and the employment and upskilling of locals (Harrison, 1992).

In Thailand alone, in the last quarter of a century foreign tourist arrivals increased tenfold, from about 600,000 in 1970 to 6 million in 1993. This growth in tourist numbers was accelerated by the development of a local infrastructure, transportation services, accommodation, and other tourism-oriented facilities. Today tourism is a high contributor to exports and the GDP in Thailand. This has attracted further foreign investment to this sector and country. To encourage this development the Tourism Organisation of Thailand (TOT, later Tourism Authority of Thailand, TAT) was established in

1959. It is this organization that is behind the recent "Amazing Thailand" promotional campaign.

The tourism industry is an amalgam of complementary services, which are offered by fragmented stakeholders from diverse industries (Gee, Makens, and Choy, 1989). Leiper (1979) suggested that we should view it as a system in which every party is responsible for, or involved in, different components of the total tourism product. This view highlights the highly interdependent nature of organizational relations in tourism. For this reason, tourism planners and scholars need to consider the need for collaboration in tourism efforts if they are to be truly successful. There has, in fact, been a tremendous surge in the number and type of collaborations between tourism-related organizations. This has become a major strategy for these planners. Project initiators, however, have found that developing a successful collaborative project is a challenging task. This is partly due to the diversity of the tourism industry itself. A lack of awareness of their interdependency, unclearness about collaborative roles, and different ideologies are but some of the barriers hindering successful collaboration (Reid, 1987).

Collaboration in tourism has only more recently been addressed (for example, Hill and Shaw, 1995; Selin, 1993; Palmer and Bejou, 1995). While researchers have emphasized many different aspects of this topic, it is their overriding opinion that successful collaborative tourism efforts require a clear understanding of the conditions and motives underlying the entry of organizations into such alliances (Selin and Chavez, 1995).

This chapter examines the preconditions of tourism efforts, especially those critical to attaining tourism objectives. Using a case study of a marketing campaign, "Amazing Thailand" in 1998-1999, the authors explore the central role of the campaign convener in identifying and persuading relevant stakeholders to participate in this tourism plan.

PRECONDITIONS

A Multidisciplinary Approach

A broad review of the literature shows that a variety of theories, including exchange theory (Levine and White, 1961), strategic management (Astley, 1984), microeconomics (Heide, 1994), resource dependency (Grandori and Soda, 1995), political theory (Golich, 1991), and sociological-psychological theories (Cartwright and Cooper, 1989) can all contribute to our understanding of why firms enter into collaborative arrangements. The different premises of these interdisciplinary studies are depicted in Table 8.1.

It is unlikely that any one of these theories can completely explain the preconditions necessary for a successful collaborative arrangement. A more holistic approach to understanding this phenomenon is therefore suggested that integrates the key preconditional factors proposed by the various theoretical approaches to collaboration (see Table 8.1). Figure 8.1 helps explain the dynamics of this process. Oliver (1990) has advocated a similar approach by integrating several theories, and then proposing five generalizable determinants of interorganizational relations: efficiency, stability, legitimacy, reciprocity, and asymmetry. Logsdon (1991) also advocates this view, suggesting that collaboration will not occur unless firms perceive high stakes and high interdependence. Stakes include factors such as efficiency, stability, and legitimacy of participants. Reciprocity and asymmetry relate to interdependency among them.

As Figure 8.1 identifies, human interactions are central to collaboration. This is because they occur between human beings (see

TABLE 8.1. Different Theoretical Bases Underlying Preconditions

Exchange Theory	Perceived Mutual Benefits
Strategic Management	Reduce threats and capitalize on environmental opportunities
Microeconomics Theory (Transaction Cost and Agency Theory)	Achieve efficiency
Resource Dependency	Lack of self-sufficiency
Political Theory	Gaining legitimation and power
Sociological-Psychological Theories	Social relationships, emotional attachment, trust and commitment

FIGURE 8.1. A Critical Preconditions Model for Collaboration

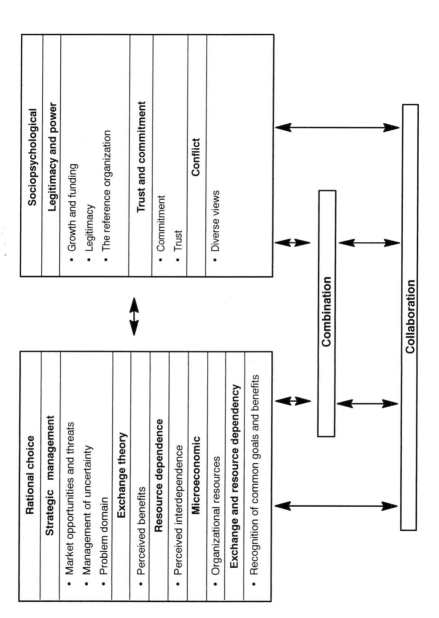

126

Cartwright and Cooper, 1989; Jantarat, 1996; Noble, Stafford, and Roger, 1995). Complete rationality in decision making is therefore unlikely and furthermore every decision is influenced by factors that are dynamic as well as heavily interrelated. This means that researchers need to incorporate the situation-specific interpretations of participants and their enforcing effects on studies of any relationships. To better capture the dynamism and complexities of collaboration we, therefore, propose a model of critical preconditions for successful collaborative tourism marketing (see Figure 8.1). This model allows for the integration of the economic-rational aspects of collaboration,[1] although it highlights relationship effects.

From this dynamic and multidisciplinary perspective, the procedural and highly interactive nature of collaboration is more obvious. The model identifies how participating firms' past experiences, their perceptions of the benefits to be obtained from collaboration, and their assessment of likely future relations impact decision making. Furthermore, it acknowledges the situation-specific nature of managerial actions, as well as its cumulative effects. This means that collaborative relationships are the sum of perceived *past, present,* and *future* benefits. Essentially, collaboration will be enhanced when stakeholders have positive past experiences and trust in the collaborative initiator and/or convener's ability to achieve the goals of the collaborative project. These issues need to be understood by conveners and conveyed to participants if collaborative ventures are to succeed, for domain focus and consensus will further facilitate collaboration.

Collaboration in tourism marketing must also provide participants with greater perceived benefits and opportunities than any individual action would (Jantarat, 1996). This indirectly has the effect of attracting other supporters and participants. Situations such as economic recessions and demand uncertainty, in particular, create impetus for joint tourism initiatives. It should be recognized, however, that perceptions of the benefits to be had from joint efforts may vary considerably across participants and may include marketing economies, access to tourism information, increased demand, and technological assistance. Finally, the model suggests that managers may not understand or believe that their current involvement in a collaborative campaign has any significant attraction. They, nevertheless, are party to activities because of future potential gains, which may include legitimization and enhancement of their image (Jantarat, 1996).

The proposed model highlights the importance of a referent or convening organization for successful collaborative efforts. The convener commonly identifies and approaches potential partici-pants, explains to them the proposed campaign, and requests their support. A recent study of a tourism marketing event (Jantarat, 1996) additionally pointed to the importance of such an organiza-tion communicating the potential benefits to be obtained from joint involvement to would-be participants. Tourism managers in this study were also found to have divergent opinions about the planned event. Difficulties in achieving a collaborative solution are there-fore directly related to differences in value orientations, as well as strong vested interests. This situation stresses the need for a con-vening organization to provide strong leadership and direction, an appreciation of trends and issues, as well as infrastructural support.

The following case study, the 1998-1999 "Amazing Thailand" campaign, examines the dynamics of the role of such a champion organization in the developmental stages of a tourism collaboration. It is hoped this investigation will further the tourism industry's understanding of preconditions that are critical for the continued growth of their industry, especially in developing economies.

CASE STUDY: AMAZING THAILAND

In 1997, the Tourism Authority of Thailand (TAT), the central governmental tourism organization, began a national marketing plan to boost national earnings from tourism. This campaign was envisaged as part of an overall government effort to recover from the Thai economic downturn. Specifically, the major objectives of the plan were to increase foreign visitor arrivals to 17 million in 1998-1999 and to return 600,000 million baht in foreign exchange over this time.

Using the catchword "Amazing," the TAT designed a marketing campaign that covered many aspects of the tourism products and services sought by international visitors. Nine themes were identi-fied:

- Amazing shopping paradise
- Amazing tastes of Thailand
- Amazing culture and heritage
- Amazing world heritage
- Amazing natural heritage
- Amazing Thai arts and lifestyle
- Amazing sports
- Amazing agricultural produce
- Amazing gateway

Pradech Phayakvichien, Deputy Governor of TAT, was appointed as a project manager to facilitate initiated cooperative efforts, which began with in-house development of the campaign. Five different groups of organizations related to the tourism industry were then identified that TAT believed should take part in the campaign. These stakeholders[2] were classified as media groups, tourism industry associations, governmental bodies, and community groups. These organizations were then invited by mail to attend the first formal presentation of the campaign.

The campaign was first officially announced on June 2, 1997, at the Queen Sirikit National Convention Centre by the minister to the prime minister's office, Piyanat Watcharaporn, together with TAT Governor Seree Wangpaichitr and other senior officials. Seree told invited industry representatives that the campaign was one way the industry could help the nation's economy, which by late 1997 had been hit by a financial crisis that had enveloped much of Asia. Acknowledging that many organizations were adversely affected by the regional economic downturn, Seree called for a joint national tourism planning approach to the problem.

A second meeting, between the TAT and identified stakeholders, was held on August 13, 1997. Forty shareholder groups were present at this meeting. The main objectives were to discuss details of the planned program and to encourage stakeholders to support the campaign. They were asked to submit their proposals of their involvement with TAT before September 15, 1997. It was also suggested that proposals highlight major festivals and events as part of the campaign. Understanding the nation's economic crisis, TAT also suggested interested participants make only minor modifications to their existing organizational strategies. Managers were asked to include the Amazing Thailand logo and concept in all of their upcoming promotional plans. This approach was well accepted by all managers. Many actually noted that by adopting this theme and coordinating their efforts nationwide, they would be more likely to attract international tourists' attention.

Following the second meeting to discuss Amazing Thailand called by the TAT, more informal talks were held between TAT officials and selected stakeholders. The manager of the campaign spoke with key stakeholders individually to elicit their support for the project. Individuals spoken to included managers from Thai Airways and Star Alliance, the National Chamber of Commerce, the local transportation association, the Kodak and Fuji film companies, Telecom Asia, the Hotel Association, and department store officials. A number of informal discussions were held on an ongoing basis with these key stakeholders. This was done to encourage further collaborative initiatives among stakeholders. Finally, the first Amazing Thailand activities and shows took place between December 27, 1997, and January 4, 1998, at Sanam Luang, Bangkok.

THE RESEARCH

The 1998-1999 Amazing Thailand campaign proposed by the TAT was used to explore the role of a convening organization. Two months after the grand opening of the campaign, semistructured interviews were conducted with key TAT officials using open-ended questions. The national and a regional governor of TAT were also interviewed. Details about the proposed campaign and the formation of the collaborative plan were discussed.

After interviews with key TAT officials were completed, the researchers arranged meetings with managers from ten participating organizations. Discussions focused on the role of the TAT in implementing the proposed campaign and the perceptions of each manager about this initiative, as well as their motives for involvement in the campaign. Managers were carefully selected to ensure a variety of businesses and views were represented. The gathered data was then cross-checked with archival and secondary data, such as meeting reports and project proposals.

Information from interviews and related documents was then aggregated and analyzed using content analysis (Krippendorff, 1980). Preliminary findings were then discussed with interviewees to clarify emerging patterns and for validation purposes.

PERCEPTIONS OF THE CONVENER

The TAT was the initiating and prime driving force behind this nationwide tourism promotion effort. They developed the concept of Amazing Thailand as a theme to market the diverse tourism products of Thailand. It was, thus, a top-down plan that was presented to stakeholders as a conceptual package when they launched their idea and campaign to participants in June 1997. It was a careful and sequential process. In the first stage, the proposal was formally presented to representatives of national stakeholder groups at a meeting chaired by the minister to the prime minister's office. As TAT acknowledged, this was done to signal to industry representatives the importance of the meeting and to legitimize their proposal. This meeting focused on what Amazing Thailand hoped to achieve for the country and for individual organizations. It also stressed that their support was vital.

In the second phase of TAT's rollout strategy for the campaign, they informally approached key stakeholders to further encourage their participation. TAT management stated that without this initiative the project would have been hard pressed to get representatives of other organizations to support their cause. As Wood and Gray (1991) have observed, representatives of stakeholder groups act as channels or gatekeepers to a secondary level of potential collaborators. Careful identification of "key" stakeholders and a major effort to involve them was seen as an important step in the successful implementation of the campaign. As Westley and Vredenburg (1991) also pointed out, although a low number of participating stakeholders was unlikely to be the sole reason for an alliance's failure, the lack of involvement by some key stakeholders was pivotal and would contribute greatly to any collaboration's downfall.

TAT managers were explicit that their personal persuasion and negotiation skills encouraged participating managers to endorse and support this nationwide tourism campaign. They further commented that they needed to clearly articulate to individual stakeholders the industry-wide and national benefits that could be obtained from their involvement. Amazing Thailand, thus, provided unity under a common branding strategy. TAT management pointed out various critical factors a convening organization needed to achieve to be persuasive. They suggested holding formal authority was important, as was having credibility, knowledge of the problem domain, and knowledge of stakeholder interrelationships. When a collaborative alliance is the convener's own idea, he or she needs to come up with convincing and credible arguments to encourage participation (Wood and Gray, 1991).

The proposal was not without its critics. In the formal and informal meetings held with key stakeholder groups and with the forty representatives, there was major concern about the name of the campaign. "Amazing" was considered inappropriate by some because of its twofold meaning. As one manager explained, "Tourists could be negatively 'amazed' by our traffic jam in Bangkok." TAT officials, nevertheless, stated that open discussions allowed stakeholders to air their views so that eventually a consensus could be reached. It was further stressed by TAT managers that their role was still far from over. Once the initial meetings were held and confidence in the project had been established, their objective was then to sustain the enthusiasm and support for the campaign that had begun to develop. This they achieved by periodic contact with stakeholder groups, as well as in-house evaluations of the campaign as it progressed.

Stakeholder Views

In-depth interviews with ten managers, representing tourism-related organizations and associations involved in the campaign, revealed many common expectations about the role of the convener in relation to the proposal. Representatives agreed with TAT that the campaign was of direct and indirect benefit to many in Thailand, including those outside and inside the industry and those present at the meeting. They commented, however, that the current economic downturn in Thailand and other Asian countries could have a negative impact on the campaign in terms of a possible decrease in the number of foreign tourists from major Asian markets. They fully supported TAT's realistic approach, especially for not asking any organizations to make major changes to their current marketing strategies. Stakeholders were additionally firm in their belief that the success of the campaign rested largely with TAT officials and government support, since TAT developed the campaign and the government had the authority to provide funding. They further believed that TAT should be granted more power and that it should be upgraded into a ministry to give it maximum administrative control of its activities.

The personal charisma of individual TAT officials was also considered as important by some managers. They further stressed that their personal relationship with TAT officials contributed to their decision to endorse the campaign and that any convening organization manager should have good communication and interpersonal skills. This latter point was considered critical as convening organizations, such as TAT, needed to create strong social bonds between stakeholder groups. This meant it was important for them to provide further avenues for formal and informal meetings between participants so they could develop a sense of shared responsibility and common purpose. Such meetings, one manager stated, could help to provide further opportunities for parallel ventures to support the main campaign.

IMPLICATIONS FOR TOURISM PLANNERS
AND MANAGERS

Despite the exploratory and limited nature of this research, interviews of tourism program conveners and stakeholders for this collaborative tourism campaign in Thailand did support the proposed critical preconditions model of collaboration (see Figure 8.1). All factors outlined in the model were considered important by stakeholders; however, the role of the convening or referent organization was perceived as critical to the project's success, both by collaborative stakeholders and the conveners themselves. There was a general opinion that convening organizations had an important role to

play in promoting the proposed campaign, in influencing and persuading stakeholders to participate, and in facilitating ongoing discussions with and between stakeholder groups about the project.

While the researchers only investigated the emergent stages of
this proposed collaborative effort, it is clear from the other comments of tourism managers and TAT officials that the role of the
TAT is far from over. Convening organizations, it was observed,
need to periodically communicate with stakeholder groups, both
formally and informally. They also need to provide opportunities
for stakeholders to interact, as well as to encourage ongoing support
for their initiative. In the former case, this may eventuate in parallel
projects that contribute to the overall success of the campaign.

It was found that an ability to communicate clearly, an ability to
exert personal influence, and an ability to understand and respond
to criticisms and concerns of stakeholder groups were believed to
be valuable characteristics for a convening organization. Personal
charisma was also identified as an important characteristic that
helped conveners to convince potential collaborative participants of
the merits of their project. An inability to convince all stakeholders
to take part in joint programs is, however, not a major issue. As
Westley and Vrendenberg (1991) observed, it is not necessary to
bring all stakeholders to the table for a project to succeed. Getting
the support of key stakeholders, those with considerable power and
influence, should be of prime consideration to the initiating organization.

While the researchers limited themselves to examining what preconditions were important to a single collaborative tourism plan, it
is possible to make suggestions for tourism managers to follow. As
Brown (1991) observed, conveners frequently face external and
internal ambivalence. We, therefore, propose a checklist of factors
to assist convening organizations in their quest for support for collaborative tourism initiatives (see Table 8.2).

CONCLUSION

Much more needs to be done to understand the dynamics of collaborative tourism efforts. This case study explored the critical embry-
onic stage of the launch of a proposed national tourism plan. Multi-

TABLE 8.2. A Convener's Checklist

---

1. Critical Convener Characteristics
   - Power to induce participation, including legitimacy and critical resources
   - Ability to communicate with stakeholders, including understanding of potential criticism as well as articulation of benefits
   - Positive personal charisma
   - Ability to understand environmental dynamics
   - Ability to envision an attractive project

2. Stakeholder Analysis
   - Ability to identify stakeholder groups
   - Ability to identify key stakeholders
   - Ability to assess factors driving key stakeholders
   - Ability to address key stakeholders' needs and concerns
   - Ability to identify other project champions
   - Ability to identify their relevant resources
   - Ability to identify past stakeholders' relationships
   - Ability to ascertain their expected future relations and goals
   - Ability to identify characteristics of key stakeholders

3. Project Evaluation and Control
   - Develop ongoing monitoring system
   - Seek stakeholder feedback
   - Conduct in-house evaluations
   - Facilitate ongoing meetings with and between stakeholders
   - Promote and encourage ongoing support

---

ple case examples and an in-depth empirical investigation would be of great value in helping to increase the success rate of such programs. Organizations such as TAT also play an important role in the development of many countries. Khandwalla (1990) calls these strategic development organizations. A closer examination of the typical tensions common in such organizations, their dependence on government for resources and direction, and their need to be creative and entrepreneurial would be beneficial for improving national development.

It is quite evident that this was a small, descriptive study. As such we can only offer guidelines for further research and thought. This campaign is also far from over, so it is too early to comment on its success. It is, therefore, important that the views of stakeholders and officials from the convening organization need to be investigated over the life of a project. We have only provided a snapshot of its early stages.

NOTES

1. Exchange theory, transaction cost and agency theory, and resource dependency and strategic management theory fall into this category.

2. Based upon Freeman's definition of stakeholder—"any group or individual who can affect or is affected by the achievement of the organization's objectives" (1984, p. 46).

REFERENCES

Astley, W.G. (1984). Toward an appreciation of collective strategy. *Academy of Management Review*, 9(3): 526-535.

Brown, L.D. (1991). Bringing organizations and sustainable development. *Human Relations*, 44: 807-831.

Cartwright, S. and Cooper, C. (1989). Predicting success in joint venture organizations in information technology. *Journal of General Management*, 15(Autumn): 39-52.

Freeman, R. (1984). *Strategic Management: A Stakeholder Approach.* Boston: Pitman.

Gee, C., Makens C., and Choy, D. (1989). *The Travel Industry,* Second Edition. New York: Van Nostrand Reinhold.

Golich, V. (1991). A multilateral negotiations challenge: International management of the communications commons. *The Journal of Applied Behavioural Science,* 27(2): 228-250.

Grandori, A. and Soda, G. (1995). Inter-Firm Networks: Antecedents, mechanisms and forms. *Organization Studies,* 16(2): 183-214.

Harrison, D. (1992). *Tourism and the Less Developed Countries.* London: Belhaven Press.

Heide, J. (1994). International governance in marketing channels. *Journal of Marketing,* 58(January): 71-85.

Hill, T. and Shaw, R. (1995). Co-marketing tourism internationally: Bases for strategic alliances. *Journal of Travel Research,* (Summer): 257-261.

Jantarat, J. (1996). Interorganizational Collaboration in tourism marketing: An analysis of critical preconditions. Thesis, Lincoln University, New Zealand.

Khandwalla, P.N. (1990). Strategic Developmental organizations: Some behavioral properties. In A.M. Jaeger and R.N. Kanungo (Eds.), *Management in Developing Countries* (pp. 23-42). London: Routledge Press.

Krippendorff, K. (1980). *Content Analysis: An Introduction to Its Methodology.* Thousand Oaks, CA: Sage Publishing.

Leiper, N. (1979). The framework of tourism: Towards a definition of tourism and the tourism industry. *Annals of Tourism Research,* 6(4): 390-407.

Levine, S. and White, P. (1961). Exchange as a conceptual framework for the study of interorganizational relationships. *Administrative Science Quarterly,* 5: 583-601.

Logsdon, J. (1991). Interests and Interdependence in the formation of social problem solving collaborations. *The Journal of Applied Behavioural Science,* 21(1): 23-27.

Noble, C., Stafford, E., and Roger, R. (1995). A new direction for strategic alliance research in marketing: Organizational cognition. *Journal of Strategic Marketing,* 3: 145-165.

Oliver, C. (1990). Determinants of interorganizational relationships: Integration and future directions. *Academy of Management Review,* 15(2): 241-265.

Palmer, A. and Bejou, D. (1995). Tourism destination marketing alliances. *Annals of Tourism Research,* 22(3): 616-629.

Picard, M. (1996). Cultural tourism and touristic culture. Singapore: Archipelago Press.

Reid, W. (1987). Recreation and tourism workshops. In *Preceeding of the Symposium on Tourism and Recreation: A Growing Partnership* (pp. 41-57). Asheville, NC: Sagamore Publishing.

Selin, S. (1993). Collaborative alliance: New interorganizational forms in tourism. *Journal of Travel and Tourism Marketing,* 2(2-3): 217-227.

Selin, S. and Chavez, D. (1995). Developing an evolutionary tourism partnership model. *Annals of Tourism Research,* 22(4): 844-856.

Westley, F. and Vredenberg, H. (1991). Strategic bridging: The collaboration between environmentalists and business in the marketing of green products. *The Journal of Applied Behavioural Science,* 27(1): 65-90.

Wood, D. and Gray, B. (1991). Toward a comprehensive theory of collaboration. *The Journal of Applied Behavioural Science,* 27(2): 139-162.

Chapter 9

Growth and Development of the Cruise Line Industry in Southeast Asia

Amrik Singh

INTRODUCTION

In 1997 the North American cruise line industry grew by 8.5 percent to account for 5.05 million passengers and occupancy of 91 percent (Cruise Lines International Association, 1998). The United States is still the world's largest cruise market with an 85 percent passenger share, followed by Europe with 13 percent, and Australia and Japan with 1 percent share respectively (Cruise Industry News, 1996). Despite its infancy, the cruise line industry in Southeast Asia is rapidly emerging as one of the fastest growing international cruise markets in the world. It is not only becoming a major cruise destination but also generating a new market of cruise vacationers. From 1994 to 1998, the cruise industry in Southeast Asia has grown at an average annual rate of over 60 percent, compared to 4 percent for the North American cruise industry (PSA, 1998; CLIA, 1998). The attraction and popularity of cruising has increased among Asians, fueled by the region's historically strong economic growth, increasing leisure time, and rise in disposable income. The region has witnessed a dramatic growth in fleet capacity, entry of new cruise lines, expansion of port facilities, and

An earlier version of this chapter was published in the *Asia Pacific Journal of Tourism Research, 3*(2), 1999.

increase in cruise passengers. In spite of the challenges posed by current economic crises, there are still excellent prospects for future growth. The success of the cruise line industry in Southeast Asia will, however, depend upon the commitment shown by the public and private sectors to sustain the high rate of growth, and to promote the concept of cruising. It will require a strategy of cooperation through public-private partnerships and joint ventures among the regional countries to attract investments and to market the cruise product. In this regard, it is the purpose of this chapter to present an overview of the growth and development of the cruise line industry in Southeast Asia, to discuss the trends and challenges, and to highlight the potential marketing opportunities in the cruise sector.

OVERVIEW OF THE CRUISE LINE INDUSTRY IN SOUTHEAST ASIA

The Southeast Asia region comprises the countries of Singapore, Malaysia, Indonesia, the Philippines, Vietnam, Thailand, and Brunei. The Caribbean-like weather conditions are ideal for year-round cruising in the Straits of Malacca and seasonally in the South China Sea. The market is characterized as a short-haul ocean cruise market, which accounts for the largest share of cruising activity worldwide (Bull, 1996). The most popular cruises in Southeast Asia are the short regional three- to five-day cruises and seven-day cruises. Most of these cruises sail from Singapore to other regional destinations such as Port Klang, Penang, Langkawi (Malaysia), Phuket (Thailand), Medan, Jakarta, Bali (Indonesia), Hong Kong, and China. These cruises are aimed at Asians, while the longer two-week long cruises are marketed to visitors from the United States, Europe, Japan, and Australia. The leading cruise operator in the region is Singapore-based Star Cruises, which controls about 70 percent of the regional market (Lee, 1997). Other locally based cruise lines operating in Singapore include Renaissance Cruises and New Century Cruise Lines (see Table 9.1). Malaysia is served by Berjaya Holiday Cruise and Empress Cruise Lines. Spice Island Cruises is the leading domestic operator in Indonesia. It operates cruises from Bali to the surrounding Indonesian islands.

TABLE 9.1. Major Cruise Operators Based in Southeast Asia

Base	Cruise Operator	Ships	Berths[a]	Share	Cruising Region
Singapore	Star Cruises	7[b]	9,463	68.4	Asia Pacific
	New Century Cruise Lines	2	1,761	12.7	Southeast Asia
	Sun Cruises	2	1,454	10.5	Southeast Asia
	Renaissance Cruises	2	220	1.6	Southeast Asia
Malaysia	Empress Cruise Lines	1	410	3.0	Southeast Asia
	Berjaya Holiday Cruises	1	400	2.9	Southeast Asia
Indonesia	Spice Island Cruises	1	120	0.9	Indonesia
	Total	16	13,828		

[a] Estimated

[b] Includes Superstar Virgo and Superstar Leo to be delivered by 1999.

Source: Cruise Industry News, 1996; author's own research.

Economic Impact of Cruising

Despite the number of limited studies, cruising has been shown to have a major economic impact on an economy. According to a study conducted by the Singapore Tourism Board (STB) and the Port of Singapore Authority (PSA) in 1996, the cruise line industry was estimated to have contributed more than US$451 million to the Singapore economy in 1995. The industry generated US$305 million in direct spending by passengers and crews on accommodations, meals, shopping, sightseeing, local transportation, and entertainment.

The indirect impact was estimated at US$107 million while the induced impact was an additional US$40 million. The cruise industry multiplier was estimated at 1.46, higher than other comparable tourism sectors, such as air transport (1.18), restaurants (1.44), and hotels (1.54) (Lee, 1996). Similar direct and indirect benefits were identified in a Canadian cruise impact study in 1993. Cruising was estimated to have directly contributed C$142-146 million to the Canadian economy in 1993, a 15 percent increase over the previous year. Passenger expenditure on pre- and posttours contributed the bulk of cruise expenditures (Gary Dukes and Associates, 1994).

Dwyer and Forsyth (1996) have also provided some tentative estimates of the economic impact of cruise tourism to Australia. The authors compared the economic impact of a six-day coastal cruise with an eleven-day international cruise. The coastal cruise was assumed to generate a higher average expenditure of A$825 compared to A$401 for the international cruise. In particular, the authors noted cruise tourists to have higher average daily expenditures (A$401) than other categories of international tourists to Australia (A$79). Cruise expenditures would also increase with the addition of precruise and postcruise packages. The authors also noted that basing cruise ships in home ports and promoting fly/cruise packages to inbound tourists would provide the greatest potential for increasing cruise tourism expenditures. These findings confirm the potential of the cruise industry to make a significant contribution to the economies of Asian countries. Therefore, it deserves national recognition and the support of the public and private sectors to ensure its viability and growth.

Attraction of Cruising

The attraction of Southeast Asia lies in the diversity of its exotic cultures and destinations, year-round warm weather, and close proximity to neighboring countries. Further, the emergence of new destinations in China, Indonesia, and Vietnam have created opportunities for new cruise itineraries. For example, aside from Bali, newly emerging Indonesian ports in Sumatra, Pulau Seribu, and Semarang are becoming increasingly popular with U.S.-based cruise lines as part of their Far East itinerary. Cruising provides a new vacation alternative for Asians who are increasingly demanding better lifestyle products. It is a convenient and affordable all-inclusive product that can be individualized to local tastes. Cruising maximizes the value of leisure time when it offers learning experiences through fun-filled activities, along with the opportunity to visit exotic destinations. Varied itineraries, competitive prices, the high quality of locally based ships, and attractive value for money cruise packages are the driving forces behind the interest in cruising (Moscardo et al., 1996; Marti, 1995). Innovations in new ship designs, high quality of food and service, and themes and activities allow Asian cruise lines to create a sharply defined product targeted at new market segments (Hobson, 1993). Compared to other types of vacations, cruising has the highest product satisfaction rate, which results in a high incidence of repeat travel (CLIA, 1998; Hobson, 1993). The CLIA Cruising Dynamics Study found that two-thirds of first time and frequent cruisers rate cruising as better than other vacation alternatives. Relaxation, pampering, choice of different geographic destinations, value for money, and variety of activities were rated as the top five reasons for its competitive advantages (CLIA, 1998). More specifically, the ship itself is a complete floating destination that offers first-class resort facilities and amenities that rival those of land-based resorts. Moscardo et al. (1996) also noted that cruises offered travelers unique experiences by combining elements from several other holiday types. Further, the study suggests that the development of cruising within a region has the potential of creating new markets. New and emerging markets for the Southeast Asian cruise industry would include South Korea, China, Vietnam, Thailand, Indonesia, and the Philippines.

TRENDS IN THE SOUTHEAST ASIAN CRUISE LINE INDUSTRY

Cruising in the region began in the early 1980s when a German-built ship, the *Princess Mahsuri,* offered a series of fourteen-day cruises to Malaysia, Thailand, and Indonesia. The ship failed to entice locals and foreigners and thereafter ceased operations. A similar itinerary onboard another ship, the *Rasa Sayang,* also ended in failure when the ship was destroyed in a fire at Port Klang. Aside from small domestic operators, cruising in the region since then had been characterized by seasonal cruises, and around-the-world extended cruises operated by the major North American cruise lines as part of their Far East itinerary. The majority of these cruise lines are in the ultra luxury category, including Cunard, Silversea Cruises, Crystal Cruises, Radisson Seven Seas, Star Clipper, and Seabourn Cruise Line.

The emergence of a rising new middle class of affluent travelers in the early 1990s had radically changed the fortunes of the cruise industry. The STB and PSA recognized the tremendous potential of cruising created by the increase in demand for international travel and subsequently began to aggressively develop and promote the cruise industry. The basic infrastructure was already in place but needed further expansion and upgrading to accommodate larger cruise ships. The cooperative endeavor and aggressive marketing by both agencies culminated in the opening of a US$35 million world class passenger cruise terminal in 1992. Major tour operators and cruise lines were encouraged to develop fly/cruise packages and to use Singapore as a hub for international and regional cruises. Singapore, by virtue of its strategic location, has developed into a major international cruise hub and a convenient gateway to the East.

Major Cruise Passenger Markets

One of the key factors driving growth has been the ability to cater to the middle class Asian traveler who makes up an estimated 85 percent of the passenger cruise market. Singapore, Hong Kong, and Malaysia account for the lion's share of the regional cruise market. Of the close to one million passengers recorded by Singapore in 1996, 83 percent were from Southeast Asia. Europe and the United States accounted for 5 percent and 4 percent of the cruise passengers respectively, followed by Australia and New Zealand with 3 percent, and Taiwan and Japan making up the rest (PSA, 1997). According to the CLIA, some 85,000 North Americans took cruise vacations in Asia in 1996 (Huie, 1996). Although they made up a small share of the overall market, the U.S. market is nevertheless expected to grow at a modest rate over the long term.

Increase in Ship Calls/Passengers

Port Klang (Malaysia), Vietnam, and Singapore, have benefited substantially from the increase in cruise traffic (see Tables 9.2 and 9.3). Together with the new Kuala Lumpur International Airport at Sepang, Port Klang is being developed into another convenient fly/cruise hub, which is expected to increase the convenience of cruising in the region.

Cruise ship calls at the Singapore Cruise Center have grown by an average rate of over 40 percent since 1991 (see Table 9.3). Despite a slight decline in 1993, the number of ship calls and passengers in Singapore rebounded in 1994 and 1995. Toward the end of 1995, Singapore imposed a regulation limiting nondestination cruises to 30 percent of total cruises over a three month period (Ng, 1996). The ruling was an attempt to curb excessive gambling

TABLE 9.2. Cruise Traffic in Selected Southeast Asian Destinations

Port	Year	Passengers	% Change
Malaysia	1992	14,700	—
(Port Klang)	1993	137,344	834
	1994	256,043	86
Vietnam	1993	4,290	—
(Saigon)	1994	6,730	36
	1995	12,286	45
Indonesia	1993	16,927	—
	1994	27,652	63
	1995	132,837	380
	1996	214,175	61

Sources: Klang Port Authority; Saigon Immigration Reports, Directorate-General of Sea Communications, Indonesia.

TABLE 9.3. Singapore Cruise Statistics

Year	Number of Ships	Ship Calls		Passenger Volume	
		Number	% Change	Number	% Change
1987	24	172	129.3	59,730	72.9
1988	23	143	-16.9	64,153	7.4
1989	30	123	-14.0	59,078	-7.9
1990	32	143	16.3	62,585	5.9
1991	29	276	93.0	131,491	110.1
1992	40	350	26.8	190,031	44.5
1993	38	344	-1.7	164,629	-13.4
1994	49	986	186.6	703,377	327.2
1995	54	1,701	73.1	933,249	32.7
1996	57	1,301	-23.8	794,357	-14.9
1997	51	1,279	-1.7	787,125	-0.9

Source: PSA, 1997.

and illegal money lending. Instead of focusing on providing a vacation experience, nondestination cruises were gaining an unsavory reputation for being nothing more than floating casinos.

As a result, some cruise lines such as New Century Cruise Lines had to redeploy their ships to Malaysia. This led to a reduction in the number of ship calls in 1996 to 1,301, while passenger volume declined 15 percent to account for 794,357 passengers (PSA, 1997). Almost three-fourths of ship calls to Singapore were multidestination cruises, reflecting an increasing profile of the region's exotic cruise destinations. As a result of the regional economic crisis and atmospheric haze caused by forest fires in 1997, the number of ship calls and passengers declined slightly by 1.7 percent and 0.9 percent respectively (PSA, 1998). Other factors blamed for the decline include a fire onboard the *Superstar Gemini* and the ceasing of operations of Lines International's *MS Nautican,* stemming from gambling-related charges. Nevertheless, the ability of the cruise sector to weather the economic crisis is an indication of its ongoing resilience, strength, affordability, and an increasing popularity of cruising.

Other ports in the region have also recorded an increase in the cruise business although growth has been achieved from a small base. In 1996, Danang (Vietnam) recorded 17,500 passengers on board 36 cruise ships, a 94 percent increase over 1995 (Racette, 1997). After years of adverse and volatile political conditions, threats of terrorism, and local shipping incidents, the Philippines recorded a 49 percent increase in cruise arrivals to 29,982 in 1996 (Bharathi, Dhar, and Gaborni, 1997).

Increase in Capacity and Fleet Size

The growth in cruising has been supported by an increase in capacity as cruise lines invest heavily in new ships to meet increasing demand from travelers (Peisley, 1995). As part of its aggressive expansion plans, Star Cruises acquired three ships, the *Golden Princess* (renamed *Superstar Capricorn*), the *Sun Viking* (renamed *Superstar Sagittarius*) from Royal Caribbean Cruises, and the five-star all-suite *Europa* (renamed *Megastar Asia*) from Hapag-Lloyd (Hand, 1997). More recently, Star Cruises sold the *Superstar Sagittarius* and chartered the *Superstar Capricorn* to Hyundai Merchant

Marine of Korea. Star Cruises has also taken delivery of its first of two 75,000-ton luxury 2,400-passenger megaliners (*Superstar Leo*), with the second ship (*Superstar Virgo*) scheduled for delivery in 1999 (Chan, 1998). Both ships will be deployed in Asian waters to provide regional cruises out of Singapore.

With those acquisitions and orders, Star Cruises has emerged as the fifth largest cruise line in the world with a fleet of seven ships and a capacity of over 9,000 berths. Star Cruises has also signed a letter of intent for an additional two 85,000-ton "Libra class" ships to be delivered in 2000 and 2002. By the year 2000, Star Cruises expects to accommodate over a million passengers, double the estimated half-million passengers handled in 1996 (Huie, 1996). Another Singapore-based cruise operator, New Century Cruise Lines has acquired the 690-passenger *MV Amusement World* to ply the Straits of Malacca, offering nondestination cruises. Sun Cruises is also planning to add a larger vessel to its fleet to replace the 1,400 passenger *Sun Vista,* which will be repositioned in India to serve the winter destination market from Europe. Ship acquisition activity is not only evident among regional cruise operators but also among domestic operators. For example, in Indonesia, Spice Island Voyages acquired the 120-passenger *Oceanic Odyssey* from Japan's Showa Lines for deployment on domestic cruises to various Indonesian islands.

More recently, Spice Island Cruises agreed to sell the *Oceanic Odyssey* to Clipper Cruise Lines. The overall increase in fleet capacity is expected to provide vacationers with a wider choice of new itineraries and increase the popularity of cruising in the region. The increase in the demand for intraregional travel and the rapid growth of cruising has also attracted new cruise operators from Japan and Singapore.

Japan's domestic cruise lines have ventured into the Southeast Asian market by offering two-week long regional cruises aimed at the Japanese market. These cruise lines include Nippon Yusen Kaisha (NYK) Lines, Japan Cruise Lines, and Mitsui OSK. Joining the competition is a new cruise line, Sun Cruises, operated by Metro Holdings, a property retail concern in Singapore. Together with its partner, Sembawang Maritime, the company acquired the luxury cruise ship *SS Meridien* (renamed *Sun Vista*) and the all-suite *Renaissance V* (renamed *Sun Viva*) (Hand, 1997).

Expansion of Port Infrastructure

New cruise terminals are being constructed while others are in various stages of upgrading at ports throughout the region. Projects include include Star Cruises' multimillion dollar investments in Port Klang, Langkawi, the redevelopment of Penang Port (Malaysia), and the construction of a world-class jetty at Bali. The Star Cruise terminal at Port Klang is fully operational and boasts the longest dedicated cruise berth in the region, capable of handling up to four cruise ships at any given time including the new megaships. In the Philippines, a new passenger terminal is being built at South Harbor in Manila as part of a joint venture between the Philippines Ports Authority, the Philippines Gaming Corporation, and the private sector.

The port of Danang (Vietnam) has also invested US$8 million on infrastructure improvements at the port, allowing it to handle up to three cruise ships at a time (Racette, 1997). A new terminal at Ho Chi Minh City will increase the number of ports in Vietnam that are capable of handling cruise ships.

With the expansion, Vietnam could emerge as the next largest growth market for regional cruises in Asia. Despite tough economic times in Thailand, the Tourism Authority of Thailand is also urging the Thai government to build a pier in Phuket to strengthen the island's potential as a regional cruise center. Singapore's investment in its cruise infrastructure is a concerted multiagency effort in line with STB's plans to develop Singapore into a cruise capital. The Singapore Cruise Center was further upgraded and expanded to accommodate the new megaships by the end of 1998. The US$15.7 million project will increase its annual handling capacity from 900,000 to 1.3 million passengers (PSA, 1997). The expansion will further strengthen Singapore's position as a hub for international cruise lines and attract more cruise operators to base their ships in Singapore.

CHALLENGES FACING THE CRUISE INDUSTRY

Being a relatively new vacation concept in the region, the cruise line industry in Southeast Asia is still faced with some challenges related to the economic crisis, infrastructure, logistical and operational issues, and a general lack of awareness in some Asian countries. The following section provides a basic discussion of the challenges facing the cruise industry.

Implications of Asian Economic Crisis

In the ongoing economic crisis, cruise cancellations were reported to be much higher for the international cruise market than in the regional Southeast Asian market. Higher cost of operations and decrease in passenger load factors, for example, forced Philippines-based domestic cruise operator, Mabuhay Holiday Cruises, to cease operating the 440-passenger vessel *MV Mabuhay Sunshine*. The economic crisis also affected Indonesia's Awani Dream Cruises, which sold its two ships, the *Awani Dream I* and *II* to Royal Olympic Cruises of Greece.

The negative impact of the economic crisis was minimal enough to prevent any major setbacks to the cruise lines, primarily due to the low prices and affordability of cruise packages. Sun Cruises, which launched its first vessel in December 1997, was reported to have sailed with an estimated 85 percent occupancy during its first year of operation (Rashiwala, 1998). Major cruise lines, such as Cunard, are staying on course for more expansion in Asia. Star Cruises suffered major cancellations when the haze first hit the region, but subsequently recovered as the haze wore on. In response to the economic crisis, Star Cruises has reduced costs by downsizing and consolidating its shore offices in the region. In addition, the line has improved efficiencies through purchasing and diversifying its customer base by attracting more Europeans and Americans. The improvements are reflected in its financial results for the first half of 1998 when it reported after-tax profits of US$17 million, an 8 percent increase over the same period in 1997 (Fernandez, 1998).

Infrastructure Constraints

With the exception of Singapore and Port Klang, port infrastructure in the region is still considered to be largely inadequate to handle the new and larger ships entering into service. The lack of dedicated passenger terminals and other facilities mean that cruise lines will continue to utilize cargo berths in many ports around the region. In some cases, the lack of support and commitment shown by the public sector has prompted cruise lines to make their own investments in port facilities as evidenced by the investments by Star Cruises in port facilities in Malaysia and Indonesia. However, the lack of port infrastructure and facilities is likely to be a short-term constraint as more port authorities recognize the contribution of cruise tourism and start planning upgrades over the next few years.

Operational and Logistical Issues

North American cruise lines still face challenges in contract negotiations, inventory management, block space agreements, ticketing, and package pricing when dealing with Asian airlines (Navarrette, 1996). Asian airspace is still very much regulated, and there are limited airline seats on high density Pacific routes. Operational differences among Asian airlines and an inclination toward protecting yields contributes to the difficulty in negotiations as well as chartering or scheduling extra flights.

In addition, the distance and long flight times to the region require cruise passengers to extend their vacation time before and after a cruise, adding to the difficulty of scheduling short cruises for the American market. The impact of this constraint is likely to be minimized over the short term with technological improvements in navigation and aircraft technology. For example, the introduction of the Future Air Navigation System (FANS) is expected to increase flight safety and capacity, while the new long-range fuel-efficient Airbus A340-500 jet will allow nonstop trans-Pacific flights, thereby reducing flight times and cost.

Education and Training of Travel Agents

Most North American cruise lines do not have offices set up in the region, so general sales agents or travel agents are appointed to represent them. In general, travel agents representing local cruise lines or U.S.-based cruise lines are not trained, equipped, or motivated to sell cruises. For example, the cruise industry in Indonesia is burdened by the lack of interest shown by travel agents in promoting cruises, stemming from the lack of support from the government. Part of the problem stems from a lack of knowledge, understanding, and benefits of the cruise product. This may be attributed to the small size and insignificance of the market, and high costs of marketing with relatively low returns and yields. Travel agents and wholesalers are expected to play a key role in the growth of cruising since a large number of agents are already well established in the region and familiar with the varied needs of clients. According to the CLIA, cruise lines rely exclusively on travel agents for the distribution of their product. An estimated 90 percent of all cruises are sold by travel agents. Cruises are also more profitable per transaction, generating an average commission of $142 compared to $98 for a land-based vacation (CLIA, 1998). As such, the high package prices and commissions, coupled with the incidence of repeat travel, make cruises an attractive product to sell compared to other vacation products. Being a major source of tourist information and a vital channel of distribution for cruises, it is imperative that cruise operators work closely with travel agents to promote and sell cruises (Hobson, 1993; Morrison et al., 1996). Familiarization trips, training, marketing support, and education can equip agents with the expertise to become cruise specialists. Once equipped with the knowledge, agents can focus on selling the product benefits, and satisfaction derived from the experience of cruising. More specifically, relational marketing will be effective in attracting, maintaining, and enhancing customer relationships.

Lack of Awareness

A general lack of awareness and misconception still exists among the Asian public about the cruise product. While some may view it as a means of pure transportation, others view it as a luxury product aimed at the affluent. Unfamiliarity with the region may account for the lack of knowledge or interest shown by the long-haul U.S. cruise lines. High port charges and shoreside costs, low yields, and low daily expenditures may also explain the reluctance of North American cruise lines to market and promote cruises to Asians.

In this regard, it is up to Asian cruise lines to adopt a proactive approach in creating awareness and educating the public on the benefits of the Asian cruise product. Cruising should be promoted as an alternative vacation choice for honeymooners, families, and other young adults. Currently, an estimated 80 percent of Star Cruises' passengers are below fifty years of age, largely made up of families, followed by mature adults and young romantics. These passengers represent the new middle class of young Asians demanding a better lifestyle, convenience, and affordability (Hamdi, 1996).

MARKETING OPPORTUNITIES

Part of the industry's success has been the ongoing marketing efforts to match its customers with the product, to understand their preferences, and to respond to their needs. Cruise lines have to Asianize their product by identifying market needs and building ships to match those needs. This may include adjusting their itineraries and providing a variety of activities, preferences, entertainment choices, and interests to meet Asian expectations as well as to reflect the cultural character of the region. The cruise product can be adapted to suit Asian passenger needs by providing more space for families, better accommodations, children's centers, fitness facilities, shopping, theme events, and enrichment programs. For example, Star Cruise ships feature locally popular game activities such as table tennis, badminton, karaoke, and mahjong. Dining options include popular Chinese and Japanese cuisine along with other regional fare while entertainment is provided by international performing artists from Hong Kong and Taiwan.

The marketing and promotion of cruises will require the cooperation of both the private and public sector to increase the demand for cruise travel. National tourist organizations such as the STB are seeking to cooperate with other Asian countries to jointly develop and promote the cruise industry. International marketing segmentation will be a key factor in creating demand for the cruise product. The cultural diversity and ethnicity of markets in Southeast Asia require cruise lines to employ market segmentation strategies to target specific groups of visitors from each Asian source market. Segmentation variables can include demographics, psychographics, vacation attributes, benefits, and first time versus repeat cruisers.

Key market segments that provide strong growth potential include the family market, repeat cruisers, corporate meetings and incentives, and special interest cruises. Through market segmentation, cruise operators can create unique and different cruise products targeted at a specific clientele to capture a larger share of the market. By differentiating the product on the basis of an image, physical attributes of the product, service level, or location, cruise lines can gain a competitive advantage and command high yields (Kotler, Bowen, and Makens, 1996). For example, Star Cruises has designed its Megastar series of ships to appeal to a niche market of upscale mature travelers who desire a private, yacht-like atmosphere, while the Superstar ships are geared toward seasoned or frequent cruisers interested in longer voyages with multiple destinations. Morrison et al. (1996) also noted that cruise vacationers can be identified by distinct travel attitudes, trip planning characteristics, and benefits experienced. Cruise vacationers were found to have rated cruising exceptionally well on most of the key benefits experienced on trips. Cruisers also showed a strong preference for escorted tours and all-inclusive package vacations.

CONCLUSION

Cruising is still the most convenient and economical way to visit Asia. A report by Travel and Tourism Intelligence has forecasted the worldwide cruise industry to grow 37 percent and account for 8.9 million passengers by the year 2000 (Bharathi, Dhar, and Gaborni, 1997). An estimated twenty-five ships providing 45,674 berths will be added to the world fleet by the year 2000 (Cruising InfoGuide, 1998). Southeast Asia, with its rich cultural diversity, and a myriad of tourist attractions, has the potential to become a major cruise destination. The region is still perceived as being exotic, diverse, and unique, which provides a competitive advantage over the Caribbean and the Mediterranean regions. The recent economic turmoil in Asia is not expected to slow industry growth except in those markets that were severely affected by the crisis. Weakened currencies will make the region more attractive to European and North American tourists, but the Asian market will remain the region's largest customer base.

The popularity of cruising is expected to fuel the rate of private and government investments in port infrastructure, new ships, destinations, itineraries, and tourism-related services. The future development of cruise terminals and ports in the region will complement efforts to attract international cruise lines to use the region as a base for Asian cruises. In particular, the region as a whole must strive to create an environment that will encourage further growth through investments in dedicated cruise facilities and new ships. Through such investments, cruise lines will be able to take advantage of internal economies of scale, and expand and diversify the onboard product. In addition, cruise lines will be able to reposition ships to new ports that will be capable of accommodating the new megaships. Cruise operators must also analyze environmental forces and design creative and innovative strategies to overcome the challenges and adapt to the changing needs of the cruise traveler. The future success of the cruise industry will also depend on the commitment shown by the governments, cruise operators, airlines, and tour operators to make cruising succeed in Asia. Through cooperative partnerships and coordinated marketing efforts, a stronger and collective Asianized cruise product will be created so the industry can thrive and prosper. The successful cruise operator will be the one that consistently delivers quality and outstanding value to meet the changing demands of the Asian cruise passenger.

REFERENCES

Bharathi, V., Dhar, P., and Gaborni, J. (1997). Cruise Control. *Asia Travel Trade,* May, pp. 42-45.

Bull, A. (1996). The economics of cruising: An application to the short ocean cruise market. *Journal of Tourism Studies,* 7(2): 28-35.

Chan, F. (1998). S'pore to be base for Star Cruises flagships. *Business Times,* Shipping, August 6, p. 1.

CLIA (1998). *The Cruise Industry: An Overview,* Marketing Edition. New York: Cruise Lines International Association.

Cruising InfoGuide (1998). *New Ships* [Online]. Available: <http://home.ica.net/~/fatusky> [October 16].

Dwyer, L. and Forsyth, P. (1996). Economic impacts of cruise tourism in Australia. *Journal of Tourism Studies,* 7(2): 36-43.

Fernandez, F. (1998). Star Cruises sees US$350m group turnover next year. *Business Times* (Malaysia), Shipping, October 16, p. 1.

Gary Dukes and Associates (1994, June). *The Alaskan Cruise Industry Benefits to Canada.* British Columbia: British Columbia Ministry of Small Business, Tourism and Culture.

Hamdi, R. (1996). Eddy Lee—Cruising on. Travel Asia [Online]. Available: <http://www.travel-asia.com/07_12_96/stories/eddy.htm> [July 12].

Hand, M. (1997). Cruise center sees record berth bookings for Dec. *Business Times, Shipping,* December 11, p. 1.

Hobson, J.S. (1993). Analysis of the U.S. cruise industry. *Tourism Management,* 14(4): 453-462.

Huie, N. (1996). Market report: The Far East and South Pacific. *Cruise Industry News 1996 Annual,* Ninth Edition. New York: Cruise Industry News, p. 382.

Kotler, P.J.B., Bowen, J., and Makens, J. (1996). *Marketing for Hospitality and Tourism.* Englewood Cliffs, NJ: Prentice-Hall, p. 259-263.

Lee, H.S. (1997). Metro to diversify into cruise, casino business. *Business Times,* February 28, p. 1.

Lee, L.K. (1996). Destination, itineraries and the economic impact of cruise calls: The economic impact of cruise calls in the region. Speech presented at the Seatrade Asia Pacific Cruise Convention, World Trade Centre, Singapore, December 4-7.

Marti, B.E. (1995). Marketing aspects of consumer purchasing behavior and customer satisfaction aboard the Royal Viking Queen. *Journal of Travel and Tourism Marketing,* 4(4): 109-116.

Morrison, A. et al. (1996). Comparative profiles of travelers on cruises and land-based resort vacations. *Journal of Tourism Studies,* 7(2): 15-27.

Moscardo, G. et al. (1996). Tourist perspectives on cruising: multidimensional scaling analyses of cruising and other holiday types. *Journal of Tourism Studies,* 7(2): 54-63.

Navarette, M. (1996). Marketing, distribution and delivery of the cruise market: The dynamics of moving passengers from North America and Europe to cruise in Asia. Speech presented at the Seatrade Asia Pacific Cruise Convention, World Trade Centre, Singapore, December 4-7.

Ng, I. (1996). Market focus: Southeast Asia. *Cruise Industry News 1996 Annual,* Ninth Edition. New York: Cruise Industry News, p. 133.

Peisley, T. (1995). Transport: The cruise ship industry to the twenty-first century. In *Travel and Tourism Analyst,* No. 2 (pp. 4-25). London: Economic Intelligence Unit.

PSA (1997). *Cruise Statistics: Steady Growth for the Cruise Industry in Singapore.* Singapore: Port of Singapore Authority.

PSA (1998). *Cruise Statistics.* Singapore: Port of Singapore Authority.

Racette, T. (1997). Danang, where the ships are. *Travel Trade Gazette* [Online]. Available: <http//www.ttg.com.sg/ttg2/current.ire/1997/0613-19/fe06 19971304.htm> [1997, June 13].

Rashiwala, K. (1998, July). Metro to cruise ahead with $26m third ship. *The Straits Times* [Online]. Available: <http//web3.asia1.com.sg/archives/st/3/pages/sinb6> [1998, August 4].

Supply and Demand Scenario (1996). *Cruise Industry News 1996 Annual,* Ninth Edition. New York: Cruise Industry News, p. 9.

Chapter 10

Vietnam's Tourism Industry: Its Potential and Challenges

Connie Mok
Terry Lam

INTRODUCTION

The notorious Vietnam War came to the end when the United States withdrew its troops from Saigon, now called Ho Chi Minh City (HCMC), in 1973. This devastating war had caused Vietnam's economy to virtually collapse. Rarely did visitors go to Vietnam for travel or to do business in the 1970s and early 1980s. In 1986, the Sixth Party Congress of Vietnam approved an economic reform policy called the *doi moi,* designed to remove restrictions on investment by the private sector, introduce foreign investment law, devaluate the official exchange rate, and restructure the banking system. As a result, foreign visitors started exploring business opportunities in Vietnam. The introduction of *doi moi* has helped the tourism industry develop from scratch since 1987. The country's political stability has also made tourism development possible.

Nevertheless, a number of constraints hinder Vietnam's tourism development. They include poor infrastructure, lax legal systems, visa restrictions, graft, lack of accommodation facilities at international standards, lack of skilled workers and qualified management people, effects of the regional economic crisis, and overbuilding of hotels. This chapter, therefore, aims to provide an overview of today's tourism industry in Vietnam, its market potential, and challenges.

MAJOR TOURISM MARKETS

Vietnam has a high market potential to make tourism become a major industry. According to the Vietnam National Administration of Tourism (VNAT), foreign travelers to Vietnam reached 1,715,637 in 1997, growing from 600,438 in 1993, representing an upsurge of 185 percent. In 1998, tourist arrivals decreased by 11.4 percent (see Table 10.1), which was probably caused by the region's economic crisis as well as the fierce competition from neighboring countries such as Thailand and Malaysia (*Viet Nam News,* 1998).

Table 10.2 reports the major sources of foreign tourist arrivals in Vietnam from 1995 to 1998. Taiwan was ranked highest, with the largest influx of visitors into Vietnam in 1995. However, the scenario has changed. China has taken the lead since 1996, although many of the visitors from China merely crossed over the northern border of the country for a few hours of shopping. The United States and Taiwan ranked as the second and third largest markets for Vietnam in 1998. The World Tourism Organization has stated that approximately 2 million Vietnamese tourists, or Viet Kieu, located in some eighty countries, will dominate the market when they return to their homeland for a visit (EIU International Tourism Report, 1993).

TABLE 10.1. Foreign Travelers to Vietnam

Year	1993	1994	1995	1996	1997	1998
Arrivals	600,438	1,018,244	1,351,296	1,607,155	1,715,637	1,520,128
Percent-age Change	—	+69.6	+32.7	+18.9	+6.7	− 11.4

TABLE 10.2. Top Eight Sources of Foreign Arrivals in Vietnam, 1995-1998

Year	1995	1996	1997	1998
Country/City				
1. Taiwan	224,127	175,486	156,068	138,529
2. Japan	119,540	118,310	124,862	95,258
3. France	137,890	87,795	81,513	83,371

4. U.S.A.	189,090	146,488	147,982	176,578
5. U.K.	52,820	40,692	44,719	39,631
6. Hong Kong	21,133	14,918	10,696	8,573
7.Thailand	23,117	19,626	18,337	16,474
8. China	62,640	377,555	405,279	420,743

Source: International Cooperation Department, VNAT, 1999.

INVESTMENT IN ACCOMMODATION

According to Vietnamese government statistics (International Cooperation Department, 1999), a total of 56,000 hotel rooms were reported in 1997, of which 28,000 were at international standards, compared to 1993 figures when there were only 10,500 rooms (Mok and Lam, 1998). The number of hotel rooms has expanded tremendously during the last few years. However, given the decline of foreign visitors as a result of regional economic turmoil, Vietnam is facing a glut of hotels. The so-called "smokeless" industry is now experiencing a downturn in attracting foreign tourists. The average room occupancy rate has plummeted to 52 percent in Hanoi and 48 percent in HCMC in 1997 (*Los Angeles Times,* 1997). The General Administration of Tourism of Vietnam (*Vietnam Economic News,* 1999) even forecasts that hotel occupancy rates will continue to drop sharply in 1999.

It seems that there is a lack of strategic planning and control of hotel development by the Vietnamese government, and there are no accurate statistics for developers' reference. Many hotel projects have come about based purely on developers' assumptions about the demand for rooms in the cities. As a result, a glut of rooms in Hanoi and HCMC has forced the hotels to enter into a "price war" (Agence France Presse, 1995b). To overcome these challenges, the Vietnamese government started to shift investment to building entertainment parks and golf courses, while curtailing investments in the hotel industry (*Viet Nam News,* 1998).

FACTORS SHAPING VIETNAMESE TOURISM

Factors shaping the Vietnamese tourism industry are: the environment, politics, and government involvement, all of which are closely linked and crucial to the successful development of tourism in the country. Vietnam has many natural endowments and resources that are major attractions for tourists. Hanoi and HCMC are the most popular cities for visitors, as people can find elegant French architecture and boutiques, and weathered colonial buildings there. The 3,000-kilometer coastline also contains plenty of untouched scenic spots and beach resorts, which have become popular tourist attractions.

Vietnam was accepted as a member of Association of Southeast Asian Nations (ASEAN) in July 1995. According to the agreement, the other ASEAN members will provide assistance to Vietnam in terms of personnel training and development, financial support, and involvement in promotional activities, such as encouraging ASEAN-bound visitors to extend their trips to Vietnam.

In July 1995, the United States restored bilateral diplomatic relations with Vietnam. To many Vietnamese, the return of the Americans represented the return of commerce and tourism (*Agence France Presse,* 1995b). Financially, hotel investors are now able to obtain low-cost financing from banks and other financial agents, who believe that the investment environment has become less risky in Vietnam. Subsequently, newly established international hotels providing a supply of hotel rooms and an upgrading of tourism facilities are feasible and provide an impetus to tourism development.

The Vietnamese government's determination to develop tourism as its dominant foreign exchange earner cannot be underestimated. To highlight the key roles of the tourism industry and to facilitate its development, the Vietnamese government set up a new and improved Vietnam National Administration of Tourism (VNAT) in 1993. The new VNAT has established goals focusing on the need for stronger state management, strategic planning, training, and the easing of formalities for the tourism industry. Working with provincial tourism service bureaus, it also helps make plans for the introduction of new standards and licensing policies.

PROBLEMS OF HOTEL
AND TOURISM DEVELOPMENT

Although Vietnam seems to have shown signs of resurgence after adopting the economic reforms in 1986, there remain considerable obstacles and constraints that have hindered its hotel and tourism development. There is a lack of accurate statistical information about visitors, which is important for investors who wish to draft development strategies and plans. The multiplicity of organizations involved and the lack of historically reliable and timely statistics make it difficult to understand the tourism industry in Vietnam (Hobson, Heung, and Chon, 1994). Visa restrictions and the cost of their application lower foreign visitors' motivation to travel into the country. Pickpockets and robbers are common in cities, and travelers are advised not to stroll alone on streets at night. Many tourist areas have nonexistent or nonfunctional street lighting. Therefore, safety has become a major issue for travelers.

Tourism and hotel investment is hampered by a lack of investment funds from the almost bankrupt Vietnamese government. This causes investors to rely on foreign banks for loans and financial support. Should there be any sense of investment instability, it will affect financing and development projects. Fortunately, confidence among prospective investors and banks has soared in recent years, and the international financial credit for Vietnam has increased (Schwarz, 1995). Cumbersome application processes for the approval of property designs and construction permits by hotel investors in Vietnam have commonly resulted in delays to their projects. In this connection, construction costs are high. Graft is serious in Vietnamese government departments. Officials have to be bribed to expedite the application process, but this adds to operating expenses and causes construction costs to escalate (Collins, 1995). Investors are therefore cautious; they calculate the opportunity costs before putting their money into such a high-risk investment environment.

Vietnam has suffered from a high inflation rate. According to the General Statistics Office, the year-on-year rate for May 1995 reached 19.4 percent, and prices had risen 10.5 percent in the first five months of that year (Agence France Presse, 1995a). Added to this, the shortage of building materials and supplies has forced hotel developers to import cement, iron, glass, marble, and other materials, at high cost, from foreign countries. Consequently, some hotel projects have come to a halt or have been converted into offices or residences due to financial difficulties.

Vietnam has an inadequate system of business laws and policies to govern the business community. The interpretation and application of laws and decrees by different levels of government authorities are confusing, and this has undermined investors' confidence. What makes this even worse is that fast-changing rules and regulations are unclear and annoying to investors. Very often, business deals cannot be guaranteed, even when the contract has been signed by all parties concerned (Reuters News Service, 1995).

The poor public infrastructure in Vietnam is a major constraint to hotel and tourism growth in the country. Roads are poor, with many potholes. Transport links between the north and south parts of the country are inadequate. Floods in roads after downpours are very common in tourist destination sites, causing a great deal of inconvenience to tourists. The railway system is weak and substandard. Trains, still using steam engines, are slow and of poor quality. Poor transportation networks and facilities have impeded travel by international tourists within the country. Domestic air travel is operated mainly by Vietnam Airlines, but the aircraft are old and poorly maintained. Other than HCMC, Hanoi, and Da Nang, where international airports are found, other tourist attraction regions rely very much on domestic air travel. Unfortunately, a lack of capital to modernize and expand provincial airports has slowed the tourism development of those regions.

The regional economic crisis since 1998 has made Vietnam less attractive for foreign travelers. The devaluation of currencies in some neighboring countries such as Thailand and Malaysia against the U.S. dollar has made Vietnam a relatively more expensive place to visit.

CONCLUSIONS AND RECOMMENDATIONS

It is apparent that Vietnam is facing many problems in the development of its hotel and tourism industry. The Vietnamese government needs to look into several crucial issues immediately if it wishes to welcome 9 million foreign arrivals by the year 2010 as predicted (*Los Angeles Times,* 1995). The most critical issue is safety. Internally, stringent law enforcement measures must be undertaken to ensure a safer environment for tourists, especially in the major tourist regions. Police should intensify their efforts by arranging for more police officers to patrol on the streets in major tourist attraction areas; police patrols are inadequate at the moment. Sound management of tourist attractions is required to preserve and maintain heritage ruins and facilities. Although Vietnam plans to invest billions of dollars to upgrade its transport networks and other infrastructure in the next five years (*Financial Times Business Report,* 1995), improving the deteriorating drainage system in the cities should be a priority. Flooding on the streets after every downpour is common, and consequently, such bad experiences might undermine tourists' motivation to repeat their visits to the country. The current regional economic crisis has dampened Vietnam's hotel and tourism industry. Vietnam's currency did not devalue significantly when the currencies in its neighboring countries were drastically devalued, making Vietnam lose competitiveness in terms of value to travelers. Thus the major challenge that Vietnam faces today is to develop a favorable investment environment through imposing a favorable profit tax rate to help speed up investors' financial returns on hospitality and tourism projects. On the other hand, in order to attract more tourists into the country, the government may consider expediting tourist visa applications and lowering their cost. Stamping visas on arrival for tourists staying less than two weeks so that they do not need to apply more than a week ahead is one way to simplify entrance procedures. In terms of long-range strategies, the conservation of heritage and cultural remains is essential. The development of natural parks could be a point to start. Training centers and hotel schools should be established to develop employees and upgrade industry service standards, which are now inadequate.

Externally, strategic marketing planning and promotion activities are required to improve Vietnam's public image and expand its international market share. Neighboring countries such as Laos, Thailand, Cambodia, and the Philippines have similar historical and cultural backgrounds and have common tourism objectives and goals. In spite of the competitiveness in the region, Vietnam may work with neighboring countries collectively in terms of travel promotion or sharing tourist information.

Thus, instead of promoting Vietnam as a single tourist destination, it would be a great advantage for Vietnam to work with those neighboring countries to promote their destinations as a tourism package (Heung and Leung, 1996).

The recent growth in the number of tourist arrivals indicates that there is a huge potential for tourism development in the country. Although Vietnam has to face tremendous obstacles in the course of its tourism development, particularly with respect to the country's unfavorable image, its abundant human resources and the government's determination to promote tourism have laid down a good foundation for its tourism resurgence in the future.

REFERENCES

Agence France Presse (1995a). Inflation at 19.4 percent exceeds forecast. *South China Morning Post,* June 9.

Agence France Presse (1995b). Lack of planning for infrastructure and promotion deals blow to industry. *South China Morning Post,* Business Section, June 27, p. 7. *Chicago Tribune* (1995). May 1, p. 3.

Collins, M. (1995). Coping with corruption. *Asia, Inc.,* July, p. 20.

EIU International Tourism Report (1993). *Indochina-Vietnam, Cambodia and Laos,* No. 2, London: Economic Intelligence Unit, pp. 65-69.

Financial Times Business Report (1995). Asia-Pacific Telecoms Analyst. *Financial Times Business Report,* March 27, p. 17.

Heung, V. and Leung, K.P. (1996). Tourism marketing and promotion for Indo-China: The consortium concept. In Chon, K. (Ed.), *Second International Conference—Tourism in Indo-China: Opportunities for Investment, Development, and Marketing.* Houston, Texas, April 25-27, p. 87.

Hobson, P., Heung, V., and Chon, K. (1994). Vietnam tourism industry: Can it be kept afloat? *Cornell H.R.A. Quarterly 35*(5): 42-49.

International Cooperation Department (1999). Vietnam National Administration of Tourism (VNAT), Hanoi.

Los Angeles Times (1995). June 12, p. 5.

Los Angeles Times (1997). June 9, p. A-2.

Mok, C. and Lam, T. (1998). Hotel and tourism development in Vietnam. *Journal of Travel and Tourism Marketing 7*(1): 85-91.

Reuters News Agency (1995). French colonial yields to concrete. *South China Morning Post,* Business Section, July 6.

Schwarz, A. (1995). *Business—Economics,* July 6, p. 68.

Viet Nam News (April 1998). Tourism industry faces steep climb to target. <http://home/vnn.vn/english/news/special-news/tourism-industry.html>.

Vietnam Economic News (1999). Vietnam: Hotel occupancy down, January 2.

Index

Page numbers followed by the letter "i" indicate illustrations; those followed by the letter "n" indicate notes; those followed by the letter "t" indicate tables.

Vietnam *(continued)*
  recommendations, 162-164
"Vietnam by Train," 8
Vietnam National Administration
    of Tourism (VNAT)
  goals, 160
  tourism growth, 157-158,
    158t-159t
Vietnam War, impact on tourism, 157
Visas, Vietnam, 161, 163
Visit ASEAN Year, 24
Visit Thailand Year, 24-25
Vulnerability framework, 50, 52, 53i,
  54

Wangpaichitr, Seree, 129
Waste disposal, small island tourism,
  113
Watcharaporn, Piyanat, 129
Water purification, Thailand, 9
Water supply
  Kuta Lombok, 4
  of Singapore, 30
  small island tourism, 113

"White Australia" immigration
    policy, 89
Wichaidit, Tawat, 36
Wind cave, Gunung Mulu National
    Park, 43, 44
World Tourism Organization (WTO)
  revised projections, 97
  sustainable tourism development,
    40
  tourism projections, 90
  Viet Kieu, 158
  Vietnam master plan, 7
World Travel and Tourism Council,
    tourism projections, 90
World Travel and Tourism Research
    Centre (WRTTRC), 1

XVI Commonwealth Games (1998),
  4

Zetaform bay, type of coast, 109,
  110i

HAWORTH HOSPITALITY PRESS
Hospitality, Travel, and Tourism
K. S. Chon, PhD, Executive Editor

SERVICE QUALITY MANAGEMENT IN HOSPITALITY, TOURISM, AND LEISURE edited by Jay Kandampully, Connie Mok, and Beverley Sparks. (2000).

TOURISM IN SOUTHEAST ASIA: A NEW DIRECTION edited by K. S. (Kaye) Chon. (2000). "Presents a wide array of very topical discussions on the specific challenges facing the tourism industry in Southeast Asia. A great resource for both scholars and practitioners." *Dr. Hubert B. Van Hoof, Assistant Dean/Associate Professor, School of Hotel and Restaurant Management, Northern Arizona University*

THE PRACTICE OF GRADUATE RESEARCH IN HOSPITALITY AND TOURISM edited by K. S. Chon. (1999). "An excellent reference source for students pursuing graduate degrees in hospitality and tourism." *Connie Mok, PhD, CHE, Associate Professor, Conrad N. Hilton College of Hotel and Restaurant Management, University of Houston, Texas*

THE INTERNATIONAL HOSPITALITY MANAGEMENT BUSINESS: MANAGEMENT AND OPERATIONS by Larry Yu. (1999). "The abundant real-world examples and cases provided in the text enable readers to understand the most up-to-date developments in international hospitality business." *Zheng Gu, PhD, Associate Professor, College of Hotel Administration, University of Nevada, Las Vegas, CA*

CONSUMER BEHAVIOR IN TRAVEL AND TOURISM by Abraham Pizam and Yoel Mansfeld. (1999). "A must for anyone who wants to take advantage of new global opportunities in this growing industry." *Bonnie J. Knutson, PhD, School of Hospitality Business, Michigan State University*

LEGALIZED CASINO GAMING IN THE UNITED STATES: THE ECONOMIC AND SOCIAL IMPACT edited by Cathy H. C. Hsu. (1999). "Brings a fresh new look at one of the areas in tourism that has not yet received careful and serious consideration in the past." *Muzaffer Uysal, PhD, Professor of Tourism Research, Virginia Polytechnic Institute and State University, Blacksburg*

HOSPITALITY MANAGEMENT EDUCATION edited by Clayton W. Barrows and Robert H. Bosselman. (1999). "Takes the mystery out of how hospitality management education programs function and serves as an excellent resource for individuals interested in pursuing the field." *Joe Perdue, CCM, CHE, Director, Executive Masters Program, College of Hotel Administration, University of Nevada, Las Vegas*

MARKETING YOUR CITY, U.S.A.: A GUIDE TO DEVELOPING A STRATEGIC TOURISM MARKETING PLAN by Ronald A. Nykiel and Elizabeth Jascolt. (1998). "An excellent guide for anyone involved in the planning and marketing of cities and regions. . . . A terrific job of synthesizing an otherwise complex procedure." *James C. Maken, PhD, Associate Professor, Babcock Graduate School of Management, Wake Forest University, Winston-Salem, North Carolina*